The Complete Plant-Based Cookbook for Beginners

Prepare a Feast for Your Taste Buds with Tons of Quick and Delicious Plant-Based Recipes
Top Secret Cooking Tips to Cook Healthy Meals

Michael Gill

Table of Contents

The Basics of a Plant-Based Diet

What Is A Plant-Based Diet?

Some people are doing it; some people are talking about it, but there is still a lot of confusion about what a whole plant-based diet actually entails. Since we split food into their macronutrients: sugars, proteins, and fats, most of us are uncertain about nutrition. What if we were able to put these macronutrients back together again in order to free your mind from confusion and stress? The secret here is simplicity.

Whole foods are foods that come from the earth unprocessed. Now, on a whole food plant-based diet, we eat some minimally processed foods like whole bread, whole wheat pasta, tofu, nondairy milk, and some nuts and seed butter. All of these are fine as long as they are handled to a minimum. So here are the different categories:

- Legumes (basically lentils and beans) of whole grains.
- Fruits and vegetables
- Nuts and seeds (including nut butter)
- Herbs and spices

All categories mentioned above constitute an entire diet based on plants. How to prepare them is where the fun comes in; how to season and cook them; and how to mix and match to give them great flavor and variety in your meals. So long as you regularly eat these foods, you will forever forget about sugars, protein, and fat.

Now, some may say, "Well, I can't eat soy," "I don't like tofu," and so on. Well, the beauty of an entire diet based on food plants is that if you don't like some food, like soy, in this case, you don't have to eat it. In a whole plant-based diet, it is not a necessary component. Instead of barley, you can get brown rice, quinoa instead of wheat; I'm sure you catch the drift right now. It really does not matter. Only find the right thing for you.

Just because you decided to adopt a plant-based diet lifestyle, that doesn't mean it's a healthy diet. Plant-based diets have a fair share of junk and other unhealthy foods, case in point, regular veggie pizza, and non-dairy ice cream consumption. Staying healthy requires you to eat healthy foods – even in a dietary setting, based on plants.

A few words that fly around are a similar eating style, but they're both distinct. That doesn't mean you're going to have to tag yourself to adhere to that way of eating; these words define various ways of eating to help you understand what types of food choices are in a particular class. This analysis can also help you understand how a diet based on a crop blends into the larger picture.

- Plant-based: This way of eating is based on berries, vegetables, rice, legumes, nuts, and seeds with few or no foods of animal origin. The plant-based diet is preferably a vegan diet with some versatility in the intermediate stages, with the intention of becoming 100% plant-based over time.
- Vegan: It describes someone who eats nothing from an animal, be it fish, fowl, rodents, or insects. Vegans refrain from animal meats as well as from other animal-made foods (such as milk and honey). They also often abstain from buying, wearing or using any kind of animal products (e.g., leather).
- Fruit: it represents a vegan diet consisting primarily of fruit.
- Raw vegan: This is an uncooked vegan diet that often includes dehydrated foods.
- Vegetarian: Sometimes, this plant-based diet includes milk and eggs.
- Flexitarian: This plant-based diet includes the occasional meat or fish consumption. I like to call it "a little bit of this and a little bit of that" — said, of course, without judgment!

Why You Need To Cut Back On Processed And Animal-Based Products

You've probably heard that fast food is bad for you over and over again. "Avoid preservatives; avoid processed foods;" but no one really gives you any real or solid information about why they should be avoided and why they are dangerous. So, let's break it down so you can fully understand why these guilty culprits should be stopped.

They have huge addictive properties

We have a strong tendency as humans to be addicted to certain foods, but the fact is that it is not our fault entirely. Practically all of the unhealthy foods we indulge in activate our dopamine neurotransmitter brains from time to time. It makes the brain feel "healthy," but this is for only a short time. This also creates a tendency toward addiction; that's why somebody will always find themselves going back to another candy bar – even if they don't really need it. Through cutting the stimulus entirely, you will stop all this.

They are loaded sugar and high fructose corn syrup

Processed and animal-based products are loaded with sugars and high fructose corn syrup with a nutritional value that is close to zero. More and more studies are now showing what many people have always suspected; that genetically modified foods cause inflammation of the gut, which in turn makes it more difficult for the body to absorb essential nutrients. The downside of your body, from muscle loss and brain fog to fat gain, cannot be stressed enough if you fail to properly absorb essential nutrients.

They are loaded with refined carbohydrates

Processed foods are loaded with refined carbs and products based on animals. Yes, it is a fact that carbs are needed in your body to provide energy to perform body functions. However, the refining of carbs eliminates the essential nutrients; it eliminates the whole grain component by refining whole grains. After refining, what you're left with is what's called "empty" carbs. By spiking blood sugar and insulin levels, these can have a negative impact on your metabolism.

They are loaded with artificial ingredients

Your body treats them as a foreign object when you consume artificial ingredients. They become an invader in essence. The body is not used to accept things like sucralose or artificial sweeteners. So, your body is doing the best it can. It triggers an immune response that reduces your resistance to disease, making you vulnerable. Otherwise, your body's focus and energy on protecting your immune system could be diverted elsewhere.

They contain components that cause a hyper reward sense in your body

What this means is that they contain components such as monosodium glutamate (MSG), high-fructose corn syrup components, and certain colors that can carve addictive properties. They are encouraging your body to receive a reward from it. For example, MSG is present in many prepackaged pastries. What this does is that to enjoy the taste, it stimulates your taste buds. Just by the way your brain communicates with your taste buds, it becomes psychological.

This reward-based system makes your body want more and more, putting you at a severe risk of over-consumption of calories. What about food from animals? The term "low quality" is often used to refer to plant proteins as they tend to have lower amounts of essential amino acids than animal proteins. What most people don't realize is that more essential amino acids can be harmful to their health. Now, let's discuss more on that.

Animal Protein Lacks Fiber

Most people end up displacing the plant protein they already had in their quest to load more animal protein. This is poor because, unlike plant protein, animal protein lacks fiber, antioxidants, and phytonutrients. Fiber deficiency in various communities and societies around the world is quite common. According to the Institute of Medicine, for instance, in the USA, the average adult absorbs only about 15 grams of fiber per day relative to the 38 grams required. Lack of adequate intake of dietary fiber is associated with increased risk of colon and breast cancer, as well as disease of Crohn, heart disease, and constipation.

Animal protein causes a spike in IGF-1

IGF-1 is the growth factor-1-like hormone insulin. It stimulates cell division and growth, which may sound good but also stimulates cancer cell growth. Therefore, higher blood levels of IGF-1 are associated with increased risk of cancer, malignancy, and proliferation.

Animal protein contains high levels of phosphorus

Animal protein causes phosphorus to increase. By secreting a hormone called fibroblast growth factor 23 (FGF23), our bodies normalize the high levels of phosphorus. FGF23 was also found to cause irregular heart muscle enlargement–a risk factor in extreme cases of heart failure and even death.

Instead, given all the issues, the "high quality" of animal protein's aspect might be more appropriately described as "high risk." Like caffeine, which you will feel withdrawal symptoms after you completely cut it off, processed foods can be cut off immediately. Maybe the one thing you're going to lose is the comfort of not having to prepare every meal from scratch.

Plant-Based Diet Vs. Vegan

Mistaking a vegan diet for a plant-based diet or vice versa is quite common for people. Okay, although there are parallels between both diets, they are not quite the same. So let's really break it down quickly.

Vegan

A vegan diet is one that does not include products based on animals. This includes meat, dairy, eggs, and products or ingredients such as honey derived from animals. Someone who describes himself as a vegan carries this perspective into their daily lives. What this means is that they are not using or encouraging the use of clothing, boots, accessories, shampoos, and make-up made from animal products. For example, wool, beeswax, leather, gelatin, silk, and lanolin are included. People's inspiration to live a vegan lifestyle also comes from an urge to stand up and fight animal mistreatment and bad animal ethical treatment, as well as to support animal rights.

Plant-Based Diet

On the other hand, an entire diet based on food plants shares a similarity with veganism in the sense that it does not also promote the dietary consumption of products based on animals. It covers eggs, meat, and dairy. What's more, unlike the vegan diet, the diet does not include processed foods, white flour, oils, and refined sugars. The aim here is to create a diet of unprocessed vegetables, herbs, whole grains, nuts, seeds and legumes that are minimally processed.

The health benefits it offers are often guided by full-food plant-based diet followers. It is a diet that has very little to do with calorie restriction or macro counting, but mostly with disease prevention and reversal.

Getting Started On A Whole Food

Plant-Based Diet

Common misconceptions among many people – even some in the health and fitness industry – is that anyone who switches to a plant-based diet becomes super healthy automatically. There are plenty of plant-based junk foods out there, such as non-dairy ice cream and frozen veggie pizza, which can really destroy your health goals if you consume them all the time. The only way you can achieve health benefits is to commit to healthy foods. On the other hand, in keeping you inspired, these plant-based snacks play a role. In moderation, sparingly and in small bits, they should be consumed. So, this is how you get started on a whole plant-based recipe without further ado.

Decide What a Plant-Based Diet Means for You

The first step is to make a decision to structure how your plant-based diet will look, and it will help you transition from your current dietary outlook. This is really personal, something that varies from person to person. While some people choose not to tolerate any animal products at all, some occasionally do with tiny bits of milk or meat. Deciding what and how you want your plant-based diet to look like is really up to you. The most important thing is that you must make a large majority of your diet from whole plant-based foods.

Understand What You Are Eating

Okay, now that you have taken the decision, your next step will require a great deal of analysis on your side. What do we mean by this? Well, if this is your first time trying out the plant-based diet, you may be surprised by the number of foods that contain animal products, especially packaged foods. When shopping, you'll find yourself cultivating the habit of reading tags. This points out that many pre-packaged foods contain animal products, and if you only want to stick to plant products for your new diet, you need to keep a close eye on the labeling of the ingredients. Maybe you've decided to allow a certain amount of animal products in your diet; well, you're just going to have to watch out for foods filled with oils, sugars, salt, preservatives, and other items that might have an effect on your healthy diet.

Find Revamped Versions of Your Favorite Recipes

I'm sure you've got a number of favorite, not necessarily plant-based dishes. Leaving everything behind is typically the hardest part for most people. There's still a way to meet you halfway, though. Take some time to talk about those non-plant-based foods that you like. Think along the lines of flavor, texture, versatility, and so on; and look for swaps in the entire diet based on food plants that can fulfill what you're missing.

Build a Support Network

It's hard to build a new habit, but it doesn't have to be. Find some friends, or even family members, who are happy to be with you in this lifestyle. This will help you stay focused and inspired while also having a form of transparency and emotional support. You can do fun things like trying out and sharing with these friends new recipes or even hitting up restaurants that offer a variety of plant-based choices. You can even go a step further and look up local social media plant-based groups to help you expand your network of knowledge and support.

Getting To The Root Of A Plant-Based Diet

You'll find so many interesting things to learn and try, but I'm bringing you to the basics for now and asking you which foods to avoid.

Valuable vegetables

You'll find a whole variety of vegetables that you'll really get to know quite well when eating plant-based veggies. If you're new to this, at the beginning, you're likely to stick to tried-and-true, popular veggies because they're going to feel healthy. These vegetables are a good start:
- Beets
- Carrots
- Kale
- Parsley, basil, and other herbs
- Spinach
- Squash
- Sweet potatoes

Fantastic fruits

We all love it! You need to get on this train if you haven't because the fruits are delicious; sweet; full of sugar, color, and beautiful vitamins; and so, so good for you.
- Apples

- Avocado
- Bananas
- Blueberries
- Coconut
- Mango
- Pears
- Pineapple
- Raspberries
- Strawberries

Wonderful whole grains

Consuming whole grains of good quality is a healthy part of a diet based on vegetables. Don't worry; you can still have your pastas and breads, but the key word here is "whole." You don't want the real thing to be polished or stored. When purchasing these items, make sure that the only ingredient is the grain itself. While it is possible to purchase proper whole grains in packaging from the shelf, make sure that you double-check the label to confirm that it is indeed a whole grain (and just a whole grain).
- Brown rice
- Brown-rice pasta
- Quinoa Rolled oats
- Sprouted-grain spelt bread

Lovable legumes

Learning to love beans on a plant-based diet is important because they are a great source of food, protein, and fuel. It may take you and your body a while to get used to them, but they will soon be your friends – especially when you find out how great it is to eat them in soups, salads, burgers, and other creative media. Here are some of the best things to begin with:
- Black beans
- Chickpeas
- Kidney beans
- Lentils
- Split peas

Notable nuts and seeds

A decent handful of nuts is good. But the thing about eating them on a plant-based diet is to make sure they're unsalted, unoiled, and raw. You can feel free to eat them in moderation alongside your other wonderful plant-based foods as long as you enjoy them in their natural state. Here are the best to begin with:
- Almonds
- Cashews
- Chia seeds

- Flaxseeds
- Hempseeds
- Pumpkin seeds
- Sunflower seeds
- Walnuts

Tools & Tips for Quick and Efficient Cooking

Food processor

This is one of the most versatile tools you can possibly have in your kitchen – it can shred, chop, slice, grind, puree, and blend, all with the simple press of a button. With this machine you'll be able to make dough for your burger patties, batter for your protein bars, and a whole range of nut butters, hummus, and guacamole. In this book, you'll find several recipes that can be prepared easily with the help of a food processor.

Note: When making dough from beans and/or legumes, it is always recommended that you soak and cook dry beans, rather than using pre-cooked ingredients from a jar or can.

Food processor recipes:

Breakfasts: Paleo Power Bread, Buckwheat Protein Bread. Meals: Tempeh Split Pea Burgers, Moroccan Chickpea Rolls, Black Bean Quinoa Burgers, Tomato Curry Fritters, Spicy Lentil Burgers, Black Bean Mushroom Burgers, Mexican Chorizo Loaf. Snacks: Hazelnut Choco Plum Bites, Coconut Crumble Bars, Choco Almond Bars, Oats 'n' Raisins Cookies, Lemon Pie Bars, Almond Cookie Balls, Gingerbread Protein Bars, Peanut Butter Chocolate Bars, Quinoa Almond Cookies.

Blender

Liquid or easy-to-chew meals like smoothies or smoothie bowls are cornerstones of a plant-based diet that's high in protein and also time-efficient. The blender allows you simply to dump healthy ingredients, including protein powder, into the container with enough water and/or plant milk – and with the press of a button, you'll get a colorful, tasty smoothie in return. This tool is also heaven-sent when it comes to creating delicious soups, sauces and dips.

Blender recipes:

Breakfasts: Vanilla Protein Pancakes, Choco Berry Pudding, Chocolate Avocado Smoothie, Mango Choco Protein Pudding, Choco Almond Mousse Pudding, Gingerbread Smoothie, Orange Sunrise Smoothie, Strawberry Banana Smoothie.

Salads: Mango Lentil Salad. Soups: Provencal Lentil Soup. Snacks: High-protein Muffins, Pistachio Protein Ice Cream.

Immersion (hand) blender

The immersion blender allows you to blend smoothies, soups, stews and sauces in the pot without having to transfer the food to a separate container. It is basically a stick with blender blades that can do almost everything the regular blender can, while also cutting down on the amount of washing-up you have to do. As an extra bonus it's only small, so you can take it anywhere for food on the move!

Hand blender recipes:

All of the regular blender recipes.

Breakfasts: Paleo Power Bread, Buckwheat Protein Bread. Snacks: Hazelnut Choco Plum Bites, Coconut Crumble Bars, Choco Almond Bars, Oats 'n' Raisins Cookies, Lemon Pie Bars, Almond Cookie Balls, Gingerbread Protein Bars, Peanut Butter Chocolate Bars, Quinoa Almond Cookies.

Potato masher

If you don't have access to a food processor or blender, a potato masher makes a good cheap alternative. By channeling some human effort instead of electricity, you can easily mash ingredients into hummus, guacamole, salsa and dough for bean burger patties. A potato masher could be a lifesaver when you're enjoying a weekend camping trip and want to mash some beans, tahini and spices into a quick plant-based high-protein meal.

Potato masher recipes:

Meals: Tempeh Split Pea Burgers, Moroccan Chickpea Rolls, Black Bean Quinoa Burgers, Tomato Curry Fritters, Spicy Lentil Burgers, Black Bean Mushroom Burgers, Mexican Chorizo Loaf.

Handheld mixer

As an alternative, the classic handheld mixer can be very useful and will save you a lot of time. Preparing recipes such as Buckwheat Protein Bread, Vanilla Protein Pancakes, Protein Muffins, Oats 'n' Raisins Cookies and Pistachio Protein Ice Cream is a piece of cake with this handy kitchen device. The mixer also lends itself to whipping up some coconut cream or creating a quick tahini dressing without the risk of injuring your wrist.

Handheld mixer recipes:

Breakfasts: Buckwheat Protein Bread, Vanilla Protein Pancakes, Choco Berry Pudding, Chocolate Avocado Smoothie, Mango Choco Protein Pudding, Choco Almond Mousse Pudding, Gingerbread Smoothie, Orange Sunrise Smoothie, Strawberry Banana Smoothie. Snacks: Protein Muffins, Oats 'n' Raisins cookies, Pistachio Protein Ice Cream.

Non-stick frying pan

Last but certainly not least is the non-stick frying pan. This is a must-have for oil-free cooking as it allows you to sauté and stir-fry without the need to add any oil. With only a splash of water, onions and garlic get that wonderful sautéed aroma without any extra calories. This pan alone will help you cut hundreds of calories per day compared to the traditional sautéing method that relies on oil.

To cook completely oil-free with this pan, heat it up and add 2 tablespoons of water or vegetable stock, followed by the ingredients that you would like to sauté. Make sure to stir often and, if necessary, add an additional tablespoon of water during cooking to prevent sticking and burning.

Note that soy-based products such as tofu, TVP, soy mince and tempeh will soak up water when being cooked without oil. Compared to veggies that contain a lot of water, these ingredients will most likely need some additional liquid to prevent them from sticking to the pan. It's a good idea to use just a medium heat when frying these soy products without oil.

Non-stick frying pan recipes:

Meals: Fried Rice with Tofu Scramble, Soy Mince Noodle Bowl, Marinated Mushroom Scramble, Mac 'n' Mince, Smoky Cajun Bowl, Sweet Potato Tacos, Provencal Broccoli Bowl, Sweet Potato & Broccoli Bowl, Red Lentil Pasta, Lentil Balls Pasta, Black Pepper Tempeh Stir-fry, Chorizo Chickpea Bowl.

Breakfasts

White Sandwich Bread

Preparation time: 10 minutes
Cooking time: 20 minutes
Servings: 16
Ingredients:
1 cup warm water
2 tablespoons active dry yeast
4 tablespoons oil
2 ½ teaspoons salt
2 tablespoons raw sugar or 4 tablespoons maple syrup /agave nectar
1 cup warm almond milk or any other nondairy milk of your choice
6 cups all-purpose flour
Directions:

Add warm water, yeast and sugar into a bowl and stir. Set aside for 5 minutes or until lots of tiny bubbles are formed, sort of frothy.

Add flour and salt into a mixing bowl and stir. Pour the oil, yeast mix and milk and mix into dough. If the dough is too hard, add a little water, a tablespoon at a time and mix well each time. If the dough is too sticky, add more flour, a tablespoon at a time. Knead the dough for 8 minutes until soft and supple. You can use your hands or use the dough hook attachment of the stand mixer.

Now spray some water on top of the dough. Keep the bowl covered with a towel. Let it rest until it doubles in size.

Remove the dough from the bowl and place on your countertop. Punch the dough.

Line a loaf pan with parchment paper. You can also grease with ome oil if you prefer. You can use 2 smaller loaf pans if you want to make smaller loaves, like I did.

Place the dough in the loaf pan. Now spray some more water on top of the dough. Keep the loaf pan covered with a towel. Let it rest until the dough doubles in size.

Bake in a preheated oven at 370° F for about 40 – 50 minutes or a toothpick when inserted in the center of the bread comes out without any particles stuck on it.

Let it cool to room temperature.

Cut into 16 equal slices and use as required. Store in a breadbox at room temperature.

Nutrition: Calories 209, Fat 4 g, Carbohydrate 35 g, Protein 1 g

A Toast to Remember

Preparation time: 10 minutes
Cooking time: 15 minutes
Servings: 4
Ingredients:
1 can, black beans
Pinch, sea salt
2 pieces, whole-wheat toast
¼ teaspoon, chipotle spice
Pinch, black pepper
1 teaspoon, garlic powder
1 freshly juiced lime
1 freshly diced avocado
¼ cup, corn
3 tablespoons, finely diced onion
½ freshly diced tomato
Fresh cilantro
Directions:

Mix the chipotle spice with the beans, salt, garlic powder, and pepper. Stir in the lime juice.

Boil all of these until you have a thick and starchy mix.

In a bowl, mix the corn, tomato, avocado, red onion, cilantro, and juice from the rest of the lime. Add some pepper and salt.

Toast the bread and first spread the black bean mixture followed by the avocado mix.

Take a bite of wholesome goodness!

Nutrition: Calories: 290, Fats 9 g, Carbohydrates 44 g, Proteins 12 g

Tasty Oatmeal and Carrot Cake

Preparation time: 10 minutes
Cooking time: 10 minutes
Serving: 1
Ingredients:

1 cup, water
½ teaspoon, cinnamon
1 cup, rolled oats
Salt
¼ cup, raisins
½ cup, shredded carrots
1 cup, non-dairy milk
¼ teaspoon, allspice
½ teaspoon, vanilla extract
Toppings:
¼ cup, chopped walnuts
2 tablespoons, maple syrup
2 tablespoons, shredded coconut
Directions:

Put a small pot on low heat and bring the non-dairy milk, oats, and water to a simmer.

Now, add the carrots, vanilla extract, raisins, salt, cinnamon and allspice. You need to simmer all of the ingredients, but do not forget to stir them. You will know that they are ready when the liquid is fully absorbed into all of the ingredients (in about 7-10 minutes).

Transfer the thickened dish to bowls. You can drizzle some maple syrup on top or top them with coconut or walnuts.

Nutrition: Calories: 210, Fats 11.48 g, Carbohydrates 10.37 g, Proteins 3.8 g

Onion & Mushroom Tart with a Nice Brown Rice Crust

Preparation time 10 minutes
Cooking time 55 minutes
Serving: 1

Ingredients:
1 ½ pounds, mushrooms, button, portabella,
1 cup, short-grain brown rice
2 ¼ cups, water
½ teaspoon, ground black pepper
2 teaspoons, herbal spice blend
1 sweet large onion
7 ounces, extra-firm tofu
1 cup, plain non-dairy milk
2 teaspoons, onion powder
2 teaspoons, low-sodium soy
1 teaspoon, molasses
¼ teaspoon, ground turmeric
¼ cup, white wine
¼ cup, tapioca
Directions:

Cook the brown rice and put it aside for later use.

Slice the onions into thin strips and sauté them in water until they are soft. Then, add the molasses, and cook them for a few minutes.

Next, sauté the mushrooms in water with the herbal spice blend. Once the mushrooms are cooked and they are soft, add the white wine or sherry. Cook everything for a few more minutes.

In a blender, combine milk, tofu, arrowroot, turmeric, and onion powder till you have a smooth mixture

On a pie plate, create a layer of rice, spreading evenly to form a crust. The rice should be warm and not cold. It will be easy to work with warm rice. You can also use a pastry roller to get an even crust. With your fingers, gently press the sides.

Take half of the tofu mixture and the mushrooms and spoon them over the tart dish. Smooth the level with your spoon.

Now, top the layer with onions followed by the tofu mixture. You can smooth the surface again with your spoon.

Sprinkle some black pepper on top.

Bake the pie at 350o F for about 45 minutes. Toward the end, you can cover it loosely with tin foil. This will help the crust to remain moist.

Allow the pie crust to cool down, so that you can slice it. If you are in love with vegetarian dishes, there is no way that you will not love this pie.

Nutrition: Calories: 245.3, Fats 16.4 g, Proteins 6.8 g, Carbohydrates 18.3 g

Beet Gazpacho

Preparation time: 10 minutes
Cooking time: 2 minutes

Servings: 4
Ingredients:
½ large bunch young beets with stems, roots and leaves
2 small cloves garlic, peeled,
Salt to taste
Pepper to taste
½ teaspoon liquid stevia
1 glass coconut milk kefir
1 teaspoon chopped dill
½ tablespoon canola oil
1 small red onion, chopped
1 tablespoon apple cider vinegar
2 cups vegetable broth or water
1 tablespoon chopped chives
1 scallion, sliced
Roasted baby potatoes
Directions:
Cut the roots and stems of the beets into small pieces. Thinly slice the beet greens.

Place a saucepan over medium heat. Add oil. When the oil is heated, add onion and garlic and cook until onion turns translucent.

Stir in the beets, roots and stem and cook for a minute.

Add broth, salt and water and cover with a lid. Simmer until tender.

Add stevia and vinegar and mix well. Taste and adjust the stevia and vinegar if required.

Turn off the heat. Blend with an immersion blender until smooth.

Place the saucepan back over it. When it begins to boil, add beet greens and cook for a minute. Turn off the heat.

Cool completely. Chill if desired.

Add rest of the ingredients and stir.

Serve in bowls with roasted potatoes if desired.

Nutrition: Calories 101, Fats 5 g, Carbohydrates 14 g, Proteins 2 g

Vegetable Rice

Preparation time: 7 minutes
Cooking time: 15 minutes
Servings: 4
Ingredients:
½ cup brown rice, rinsed
1 cup water
½ teaspoon dried basil
1 small onion, chopped
2 tablespoons raisins
5 ounces frozen peas, thawed
½ cup pecan halves, toasted
1 medium carrot, cut into matchsticks
4 green onions, cut into 1-inch pieces
1 tablespoon olive oil
½ teaspoon salt or to taste
½ teaspoon crushed red chili flakes or to taste
Ground pepper or to taste
Directions:
Place a small saucepan with water over medium heat.

When it begins to boil, add rice and basil. Stir.

When it again begins to boil, lower the heat and cover with a lid. Cook for 15 minutes until all the water is absorbed and rice is cooked. Add more water if you think the rice is not cooked well.

Meanwhile, place a skillet over medium high heat. Add carrots, raisins and onions and sauté until the vegetables are crisp as well as tender.

Stir in the peas, salt, pepper and chili flakes.

Add pecans and rice and stir.

Serve.

Nutrition: Calories 305, Fats 13 g, Carbohydrates 41 g, Proteins 8 g

Courgette Risotto

Preparation time: 10 minutes
Cooking time: 5 minutes

Servings: 8
Ingredients:
2 tablespoons olive oil
4 cloves garlic, finely chopped
1.5 pounds Arborio rice
6 tomatoes, chopped
2 teaspoons chopped rosemary
6 courgettes, finely diced
1 ¼ cups peas, fresh or frozen
12 cups hot vegetable stock
1 cup chopped
Salt to taste
Freshly ground pepper
Directions:
Place a large heavy bottomed pan over medium heat. Add oil. When the oil is heated, add onion and sauté until translucent.

Stir in the tomatoes and cook until soft.

Next stir in the rice and rosemary. Mix well.

Add half the stock and cook until dry. Stir frequently.

Add remaining stock and cook for 3-4 minutes.

Add courgette and peas and cook until rice is tender. Add salt and pepper to taste.

Stir in the basil. Let it sit for 5 minutes.

Nutrition: Calories 406, Fats 5 g, Carbohydrates 82 g, Proteins 14 g

Country Breakfast Cereal

Preparation Time: 5 minutes
Cooking time: 40 minutes
Servings: 6
 Ingredients:
1 cup brown rice, uncooked
½ cup raisins, seedless
1 tsp cinnamon, ground
¼ Tbsp peanut butter
2 ¼ cups water
Honey, to taste
Nuts, toasted

Directions:
Combine rice, butter, raisins, and cinnamon in a saucepan. Add 2 ¼ cups water. Bring to boil.

Simmer covered for 40 minutes until rice is tender.

Fluff with fork. Add honey and nuts to taste.

Nutrition: Calories 160 Carbohydrates 34 g Fats 1.5 g Protein 3 g

Oatmeal Fruit Shake

Preparation Time: 10 minutes
Cooking time: 0 minutes
Servings: 2
 Ingredients:
1 cup oatmeal, already prepared, cooled
1 apple, cored, roughly chopped
1 banana, halved
1 cup baby spinach
2 cups coconut water
2 cups ice, cubed
½ tsp ground cinnamon
1 tsp pure vanilla extract
Directions:
Add all ingredients to a blender.

Blend from low to high for several minutes until smooth.

Nutrition: Calories 270 Carbohydrates 58 g Fats 1.5 g Protein 5 g

Green Ginger Smoothie

Preparation time: 5 minutes
Cooking time: 5 minutes
Servings: 2

Ingredients:

1 banana

½ apple sliced

1 orange sliced and peeled

1 lemon juice

2 big spinach

1 tbsp. fresh ginger

½ cup almond milk

For the dressing: chia seeds, apple, raspberries

Directions:

Take a blender. Peel off and slice all fruits. Add banana, apple, orange, lime juice, ginger and spinach and blend them well until they turn smooth. Now add almond milk and pulse again for a few seconds. Pour the smoothie into glasses and serve. You can add chia seeds, apple or raspberries for a smoothie bowl. Store it up to 8-10 hours in the refrigerator.

Nutrition: Calories 330 Carbohydrates 62 g Fats 6 g Protein 10 g

Orange Dream Creamsicle

Preparation time: 5 minutes

Cooking time: 5 minutes

Servings: 2

Ingredients:

1 orange, peeled

¼ cup vegan yogurt

2 tbsp. orange juice

¼ tsp vanilla extract

4 ice cubes

Directions:

In a blender, add orange, orange juice, vegan yogurt, vanilla extract and ice cubes. Blend all the ingredients well until smooth and well combined. Pour it into smoothie glasses and serve.

Nutrition: Calories 120 Carbohydrates 62 g Fats 6 g Protein 10g

Banana Almond Granola

Preparation time: 10 minutes

Cooking time: 20 Minutes

Servings: 21

Ingredients:

Organic rolled whole oats – 3 Cups

Raw Almond – ½ Cup, chopped

Sunflower seeds – ½ Cup, raw

Vanilla Extract – ½ teaspoon

Sea salt – 1/8 teaspoon

Coconut oil – 3 tablespoons, organic

Honey – 3 tablespoons, Raw

Banana – 2, ripe, small pieces

Directions:

Preheat the oven at 400F. Take a baking tray and line it with baking sheet. In a bowl, combine almonds, salt, vanilla and oats. In another small ball, combine honey, coconut oil (at room temperature), and bananas. Mash the bananas to make a smooth mixture. Now, add this banana mixture to the former dry mixture, combine until all ingredients coat each other well. Spread this mixture, granola, on the baking tray evenly. Place the tray into the preheated oven and bake it for at least 20 minutes. Check at 10 minutes interval, turn the granola upside down with the help of a spoon. Cool it down and store in a container for later use

Nutrition: Calories: 110 kcal; Fat: 5.4g; Carbohydrates: 14.2g; Sodium: 10.6mg; Protein: 2.9g

Mexican-Spiced Tofu Scramble

Preparation time: 13 m

Cooking time: 10 m

Ingredients:

1 tbsp. safflower oil

2 packages of extra-firm tofu, drained and pressed

3 scallions, chopped

2 cloves garlic, minced

1 red bell pepper, chopped

½ tsp. ground cumin

½ tsp. Mexican chile powder

½ tsp. ground coriander

½ tsp. paprika

½ tsp. garlic powder

½ tsp. dried oregano

1 tsp. black salt

2 tbsp. nutritional yeast (optional)

1/2 tsp. turmeric

2 tbsp. fresh cilantro, chopped

2 tbsp. ground flaxseed (optional)

1-4 oz. can green chiles

1 cup of water

1-15 oz. can black beans, drained and rinsed

Directions:

Heat a large frying pan over moderate heat. Add the oil and cook the chives, peppers, and garlic for about 3 minutes until tender. Break the tofu into large pieces and add them to the pan. Throw it away so that it is covered with aromatics and let it sit until it is golden before playing it. When browning after about 5 minutes, stir in the tofu to brown it on all sides.

While the tofu is browning, mix the spices in a small bowl or cup. Increase or reduce the amount depending on how you like spicy foods. Nutritional yeast and flax seeds are optional additions, but healthy if you have them. Add the spice blend to the pan and mix the tofu to evenly distribute the spices. Add 1 cup of water into the pan and stir. This helps the spices to distribute evenly and moistens the dispute. The water will cook.

Mix the green peppers and black beans in the tofu race. Cook for about 5 minutes until all the ingredients are hot. Mix the coriander. Serve hot.

Nutrition: Carbs: 91 g Calories: 1,113 Fat: 49 g Sodium: 670 mg Protein: 83 g Sugar: 9 g

Healthy Breakfast Bowl

Preparation time: 10 m
Cooking time: 10 m
Ingredients:
1 vegan yogurt
1/2 avocado (peeled and diced)
1 handful blueberries
1 tablespoon cacao nibs
1 handful of strawberries
1 tablespoon mulberries
1 tablespoon goji berries
1 tablespoon desiccated coconut
Directions:
Put the avocado in a nice bowl.
Top up with vegan yogurt.
Sprinkle the remaining ingredients and enjoy it.

Nutrition: carbs: 55 g calories: 471 Fat: 25g sodium: 183 g protein: 11 g sugar: 32 g

Root Vegetable Hash With Avocado Crème

Preparation time: 25 m
Cooking time: 10 m
Ingredients:
1/2 c onion, diced
1 T vegan butter
2 cloves garlic, minced
1 c sweet potatoes, diced
1 c turnips, diced
1 c broccoli florets, diced
2 vegan sausages, diced
1 c collard greens, chopped
1/2 tsp sea salt
1 tsp cumin
1/2 tsp black pepper
1/4 – 1/2c vegetable stock
1/4 c fresh cilantro, chopped
1 medium avocado
1 T balsamic vinegar
1/4 c cashews
Directions:

Melt and heat the butter in a skillet. Add onion and garlic and sauté until they are translucent about 5 minutes.

Add sweet potatoes and turnips stir to match. Cook for 5-8 minutes.

Add the broccoli and vegetables. Continue cooking until it turns light green and start to soften for 5 to 8 minutes.

Add the roasted field, salt, pepper, cumin, coriander, and vinegar. Reduce the heat and get it cooked until the meat is hot and the flavors melt.

Mix the avocado, cashews, and vegetable broth in a blender until smooth.

Plate and serve with a spoonful of avocado cream on top. Garnish with more cilantro.

Nutrition: 19 g fat 30 g of carbohydrates 17 g protein 7 g sugar 691 mg sodium

Chocolate Strawberry Almond Protein Smoothie

Preparation time: 10 m
Cooking time: 10 m
Ingredients:
1 cup of organic strawberries
1 1/2 cup homemade almond milk
1 scoop chocolate protein powder
1 tablespoon organic coconut oil
1/4 cup organic raw almonds
1 tablespoon organic hemp seeds
1 tablespoon organic maca powder
For Garnish:
organic cacao nibs
organic hemp seeds
Directions:
Put all the ingredients inside a blender and beat until they are well combined.
Optional: Garnish with organic hemp seeds or organic cocoa beans.
Enjoy it!
Nutrition: carbohydrates: 39 g calories: 720 Fat: 45 g sodium: 732g protein: 44 g sugar: 12g

Banana Bread Breakfast Muffins

Preparation time: 40 m
Cooking time: 20 m
Ingredients:
1/2 cup plus 2 tbs of whole oats
1/2 cup oats (processed into flour)
1/2 teaspoon baking powder
2 tablespoon vegan chocolate chips
1/4 teaspoon cinnamon
1/2 cup of a mashed ripe banana (mash the banana and then measure it)
2 tablespoons pure maple syrup
1/2 teaspoon vanilla extract
Directions:
Preheat the cooker to 360 ° F and spray a muffin pan (3-4 holes) with a non-stick spray.
Add 1/2 cup oatmeal in a food processor and beat until it breaks and forms a thick consistency of flour.
In a large container, add all the dry ingredients except the chocolate chips and mix.
Crush and mash the uneven ripe banana, add the banana and the rest of the wet ingredients to the container with the dry ingredients and mix well.
Mix the chocolate chips. Put in 3-4 muffin holes and bake for 12 minutes.
Let cool 10 mins and serve immediately or store in an airtight container for 1-2 days.
Nutrition: Per serving: Carbohydrates: 59g Calories: 347 Fat: 6g Sodium: 2 mg Proteins: 15g Sugar: 1g

Cardamom Persimmon Scones With Maple-Persimmon Cream

Preparation time: 45 m
Cooking time: 30 m
Ingredients:
For the Dry Ingredients:
2 teaspoons baking powder
1 tablespoon coconut sugar
1 teaspoon cardamom
1/2 teaspoon salt
1/2 teaspoon cinnamon
3 tablespoons softened coconut oil
For the Wet Ingredients:
1/2 cup almond milk
1 teaspoon vanilla extract
1 cup plain vegan yogurt
1 teaspoon apple cider vinegar (if you use vegan yogurt)
1 cup ripe Fuyu persimmons chopped
For the Maple Cream:
2 tablespoons shredded coconut
1/2 cup chopped persimmons
3/4 cup non-dairy milk
1/4 teaspoon cinnamon
1 tablespoon maple syrup
1/4 teaspoon salt
Directions:
For Scones:

Preheat the cooker to 400 ° F. Line a baking sheet with parchment paper or leave it bare.

Combine flour, sugar, spices, baking soda, and salt in a large bowl.

Using a fork or pasta cutter, cut the coconut oil into the mixture.

Combine yogurt, almond milk, apple cider vinegar, and vanilla in a small bowl. Add the dey ingredients to the wet ingredients and stir with a wooden spoon until the mixture is well combined. Be careful not to mix too much.

Gently fold the chopped persimmons with the wooden spoon.

Flour on a flat surface like a board or a counter. Make the dough in a circle about 1.2 cm high. Cut into 8 slices and separate.

Carefully transfer the slices to the prepared baking sheet.

Bake at 400 ° F for 18 to 20 minutes. Let cool slightly before serving.

For the cream:

Combine all the constituents in a blender or food processor.

Serve with hot scones or refrigerate for up to 3 days.

Nutrition: Per serving: Carbohydrates: 45g Calories: 264 Fat: 7g Sodium: 46 mg Proteins: 6g Sugar: 15g

Activated Buckwheat & Coconut Porridge With Blueberry Sauce

Preparation time: 10 m
Cooking time: 5 m
Ingredients:
For the Porridge:
1/2 cup coconut milk
1 and 1/2 cups soaked and washed buckwheat
2 tablespoons rice malt syrup
1/2 teaspoon cinnamon
2 tablespoons coconut oil
1/2 teaspoon natural vanilla essence
For the Blueberry Sauce:
1 tablespoon rice malt syrup
1 cup blueberries (if you are using frozen, ensure they have defrosted)
3-4 tablespoons of water or coconut water
For the Toppings:
Banana
Roast coconut flakes
Directions:
Using a high-speed mixer or food processor, mix all the ingredients for the porridge and pour it into the bowl.

Clean and mix the blueberry sauce (if not mixed well, you may need to add more water, but you don't want it to drip)

Blueberry sauce in a buckwheat porridge, and with a spoon, you can make your whirlwind.

Add toppings and enjoy your healthy breakfast!

Nutrition: Per serving: Carbohydrates: 118g Calories: 738 Fat: 26g Sodium: 24 mg Proteins: 20g Sugar: 25g

Sweet Molasses Brown Bread

Preparation time: 1 hr 30 m
Cooking time: 30 m
Ingredients:
1/2 cup molasses
1 1/2 cups almond milk, warmed
4 tablespoons coconut oil or non-dairy butter, softened
1 2/3 cups white whole-wheat flour (or regular whole wheat flour)
3 cups unbleached of all-purpose flour, plus more for dusting
2 – 3 tablespoons unsweetened cocoa powder
1/2 teaspoon ground nutmeg
2 tablespoons dark brown sugar
1 1/4 teaspoons salt
Old-fashioned rolled oats for spray on top, optional
2 1/2 teaspoons instant yeast
Directions:
Combine dry ingredients, including yeast in a large bowl, make a hole in the mixture. Add the milk, molasses, and butter and mix with a wooden

spoon until the dough is damp and unkempt, then knead by hand until the dough is thick.

Put the dough in a large bowl of oil (or leave it in a bread bucket); cover with a plastic wrap or cloth and let rise in a warm place until its size doubles, about 1 hour.

Turn the dough onto a surface that has been floured, divide it into 3 pieces, and mold it into bread.

Place the dough in a lightly greased baking sheet (or lined with parchment paper) or place it in greased forms and sprinkle with oatmeal.

Let the dough rise, protected in a warm place for 45 minutes to an hour until almost doubled in size.

Meanwhile, preheat the oven to 350 F. at the end of the rise time.

Bake for 25 to 30 mins until the color is darker , and a toothpick or tester inserted in the center comes out clean.

Remove the bread from the cooker and let cool in a rack.

Serve warm or at room temperature

Enjoy it!

Nutrition: carbohydrates: 584g calories: 3141 Fat: 63g sodium: 321 mg protein: 63g sugar: 171g

Breakfast Blueberry Muffins

Preparation Time: 15 minutes
Cooking Time: 25 minutes
Servings: 12
Ingredients:
Cooking spray
1 ½ cups rolled oats
¼ teaspoon baking soda
1 teaspoon baking powder
½ cup unsweetened applesauce
⅓ cup packed light brown sugar
¼ teaspoon salt
3 tablespoons vegetable oil
3 tablespoons water
1 tablespoon flax meal
1 teaspoon vanilla extract
¾ cup blueberries, sliced in half
Directions:
Preheat your oven to 350 degrees F.
Spray your muffin pan with oil.
Add the oats in a food processor.
Pulse until ground.
Stir in the rest of the ingredients except blueberries.
Pulse until smooth.
Pour the batter into the muffin pan.
Top with the blueberries.
Bake in the oven for 25 minutes.
Store in a glass jar with lid.
Nutrition: Calories: 106 fat: 4.6g Saturated fat: 0.4g Sodium: 118mg Potassium: 66mg Carbohydrates: 15.5g Fiber: 1.5g Sugar: 8g Protein: 1.5g

Oatmeal with Black Beans & Cheddar

Preparation Time: 10 minutes
Cooking Time: 0 minute
Servings: 2
Ingredients:
½ cup rolled oats
¼ cup Vegan yogurt
½ cup almond milk
2 tablespoons seasoned black beans
2 tablespoons Cheddar cheese, shredded
1 stalk scallion, minced
1 tablespoon cilantro, chopped
Directions:
Mix all the ingredients except the cilantro in a glass jar with lid.
Refrigerate for up to 5 days.
Sprinkle the cilantro on top before serving.
Nutrition: Calories: 47 Total fat: 1.2g Saturated fat: 0.5g Sodium: 30mg Potassium: 151mg Carbohydrates: 11g Fiber: 1.9g Sugar: 9g Protein: 2g

Breakfast Smoothie

Preparation Time: 10 minutes
Cooking Time: 0 minute
Servings: 2
Ingredients:

½ cup strawberries
½ cup mango, sliced
½ banana, sliced
½ cup coconut milk
1 tablespoon cashew butter
1 tablespoon ground chia seeds
Directions:
Put all the ingredients in a blender.
Pulse until smooth.
Refrigerate overnight.
Nutrition: Calories: 299 Total fat: 14.5g Saturated fat: 4.2g Sodium: 64mg Potassium: 599mg Carbohydrates: 42.4g Fiber: 8.5g Sugar: 23g Protein: 5.3g

Yogurt with Beets & Raspberries

Preparation Time: 5 minutes
Cooking Time: 0 minute
Servings: 1
Ingredients:
1 cup soy yogurt
½ cup beets, cooked and sliced
1 tablespoon raspberry jam
1 tablespoon almonds, slivered
Directions:
Mix all the ingredients in a glass jar with lid.
Sprinkle the almonds on top.
Refrigerate for up to 2 days.
Nutrition: Calories: 281 Total fat: 7.3g Saturated fat: 2.7g Cholesterol: 15mg Sodium: 237mg Potassium: 882mg Carbohydrates: 40.2g Fiber: 2.5g Sugar: 36g Protein: 15.7g

Curry Oatmeal

Preparation Time: 10 minutes
Cooking Time: 0 minute
Servings: 3
Ingredients:
1 tablespoon pure peanut butter
½ cup rolled oats

½ cup coconut milk
½ teaspoon curry powder
1 teaspoon tamari
¼ cup cooked kale
1 tablespoon cilantro, chopped
2 tablespoons tomatoes, chopped
Directions:
Mix all the ingredients except the kale, cilantro and tomatoes.
Transfer to a glass jar with lid.
Refrigerate for up to 5 days.
Top with the remaining ingredients when ready to serve.
Nutrition: Calories: 307 Total fat: 13.8g Saturated fat: 4g Cholesterol: 12mg Sodium: 467mg Potassium: 890mg Carbohydrates: 34.1g Fiber: 3g Sugar: 2g Protein: 10.1g

Fig & Vegan Cheese Oatmeal

Preparation Time: 10 minutes
Cooking Time: 0 minute
Servings: 1
Ingredients:
½ cup water
½ cup rolled oats
Pinch salt
2 tablespoons dried figs, sliced
2 tablespoons vegan cheese
2 teaspoons agave syrup
1 tablespoon almonds, toasted and sliced
Directions:
Put the water, oats and salt in a glass jar with lid.
Shake to blend well.
Refrigerate for up to 5 days.
Top with the remaining ingredients when ready to serve.
Nutrition: Calories: 294 Total fat: 8.5g Saturated fat: 2.3g Cholesterol: 10mg Sodium: 182mg Potassium: 362mg Carbohydrates: 47.5g Fiber: 6.6g Sugar: 16g Protein: 10.4g

Pumpkin Oats

Preparation Time: 10 minutes
Cooking Time: 0 minute
Servings: 1
Ingredients:
½ cup rolled oats
½ cup almond milk
¼ cup ricotta cheese
2 tablespoons pumpkin puree
1 tablespoon maple syrup
¼ teaspoon vanilla
1/8 teaspoon ground nutmeg
Directions:
Combine all the ingredients in a glass jar with lid.
Refrigerate for up to 5 days.
Nutrition: Calories: 344 Total fat: 10g Saturated fat: 3.8g Cholesterol: 19mg Sodium: 179mg Potassium: 364mg Carbohydrates: 51.7g Fiber: 5.7g Sugar: 16g Protein: 13.3g

Sweet Potato Toasts

Preparation time: 10 minutes
Cooking time: 10 minutes
Servings: 2
Ingredients:
2 large sweet potatoes, sliced into ¼ inch thick slices
1 tablespoon avocado oil
1 teaspoon salt
½ cup guacamole
½ cup tomatoes, sliced
Directions:
Preheat your oven to 425 degrees F.
Cover a baking sheet with parchment paper.
Rub the potato slices with oil and salt and place them on a baking sheet.
Bake for 5 minutes in the oven, then flip and bake again for 5 minutes.
Top the baked slices with guacamole and tomatoes.
Serve.
Nutrition: Calories 134 Total Fat 4.7 g Saturated Fat 0.6 g Cholesterol 124mg Sodium 1 mg Total Carbs 54.1 g Fiber 7 g Sugar 3.3 g Protein 6.2 g

Tofu Scramble Tacos

Preparation time: 10 minutes
Cooking time: 10 minutes
Servings: 04
Ingredients:
1 package tofu
¼ cup nutritional yeast
2 teaspoons garlic powder
2 teaspoons cumin
2 teaspoons chili powder
½ teaspoon turmeric
1 teaspoon salt
½ teaspoon pepper
1 tablespoon avocado oil
Warm corn tortillas
Directions:
In a pan, add avocado oil and tofu.
Sauté and crumble the tofu on medium heat.
Stir in all the remaining spices and yeast.
Mix and cook for 2 minutes.
Serve on tortillas.
Nutrition: Calories 387 Total Fat 6 g Saturated Fat 3.4 g Cholesterol 41 mg Sodium 154 mg Total Carbs 37.4 g Fiber 2.9 g Sugar 1.3 g Protein 6.6 g

Almond Chia Pudding

Preparation time: 10 minutes
Cooking time: 0 minutes
Servings: 2
Ingredients:
3 tablespoons almond butter
2 tablespoons maple syrup
1 cup almond milk
¼ cup plus 1 tablespoon chia seeds
Directions:
In a sealable container, add everything and mix well.
Seal the container and refrigerate overnight.
Serve with a splash of almond milk.

Nutrition: Calories 212 Total Fat 11.8 g Saturated Fat 2.2 g Cholesterol 23mg Sodium 321 mg Total Carbs 14.6 g Fibers 4.4 g Sugar 8 g Protein 7.3g

Breakfast Parfait Popsicles

Preparation time: 10 minutes
Cooking time: 0 minutes
Servings: 02
Ingredients:
1 cup soy yogurt
1 cup berries
1 cup granola
Directions:
In a popsicle mold, divide the berries.
Add yogurt to the molds and gently mix the berries using a stick.
Sprinkle granola on top and place the popsicle sticks in the mixture.
Freeze overnight.
Serve.
Nutrition: Calories 135 Total Fat 2 g Saturated Fat 1 g Cholesterol 2 mg Sodium 17 mg Total Carbs 33 g Fiber 1 g Sugar 13 g Protein 2 g

Strawberry Smoothie Bowl

Preparation time: 30 minutes
Cooking time: 0 minutes
Servings: 02
Ingredients:
Smoothie bowl:
1½ cups frozen strawberries
½ cup coconut milk
Chia seeds
Directions:
In a blender jug, puree all the ingredients for the smooth bowl.
Pour the smoothie in the serving bowl.

Add strawberries, banana and chia seeds on top.
Chill well then serve.
Nutrition: Calories 275 Total Fat 14.5 g Saturated Fat 12.5 g Cholesterol 36 mg Sodium 13 mg Total Carbs 25 g Fiber 5 g Sugar 5 g Protein 2.5 g

Peanut Butter Granola

Preparation time: 10 minutes
Cooking time: 47 minutes
Servings: 04
Ingredients:
Nonstick spray
4 cups oats
⅓ cup of cocoa powder
¾ cup peanut butter
⅓ cup maple syrup
⅓ cup avocado oil
1½ teaspoons vanilla extract
½ cup cocoa nibs
6 ounces dark chocolate, chopped
Directions:
Preheat your oven to 300 degrees F.
Spray a baking sheet with cooking spray.
In a medium saucepan add oil, maple syrup, and peanut butter.
Cook for 2 minutes on medium heat, stirring.
Add the oats and cocoa powder, mix well.
Spread the coated oats on the baking sheet.
Bake for 45 minutes, occasionally stirring.
Garnish with dark chocolate, cocoa nibs, and peanut butter.
Serve.
Nutrition: Calories 134 Total Fat 4.7 g Saturated Fat 0.6 g Cholesterol 124mg Sodium 1 mg Total Carbs 54.1 g Fiber 7 g Sugar 3.3 g Protein 6.2 g

Apple Chia Pudding

Preparation time: 10 minutes
Cooking time: 5 minutes
Servings: 04

Ingredients:
Chia Pudding:
4 tablespoons chia seeds
1 cup almond milk
½ teaspoon cinnamon
Apple Pie Filling:
1 large apple, peeled, cored and chopped
¼ cup water
2 teaspoons maple syrup
Pinch cinnamon
2 tablespoons golden raisins
Directions:
In a sealable container, add cinnamon, chia seeds and almond milk, mix well.

Seal the container and refrigerate overnight.

In a medium pot, combine all apple pie filling ingredients and cook for 5 minutes.

Serve the chia pudding with apple filling on top. Enjoy.

Nutrition: Calories 387 Total Fat 5.8 g Saturated Fat 4.2 g Cholesterol 41 mg Sodium 154 mg Total Carbs 24.1 g Fiber 2.9 g Sugar 3.1 g Protein 6.6 g

Pumpkin Spice Bites

Preparation time: 10 minutes
Cooking time: 0 minutes
Servings: 2
Ingredients:
½ cup pumpkin puree
½ cup almond butter
¼ cup maple syrup
1 teaspoon pumpkin pie spice
1⅓ cup rolled oats
⅓ cup pumpkin seeds
⅓ cup raisins
2 tablespoons chia seeds
Directions
In a sealable container, add everything and mix well.

Seal the container and refrigerate overnight.
Roll the mixture into small balls.
Serve.

Nutrition: Calories 212 Total Fat 11.8 g Saturated Fat 2.2 g Cholesterol 23mg Sodium 321 mg Total Carbs 14.6 g Fibers 4.4 g Sugar 8 g Protein 7.3g

Lemon Spelt Scones

Preparation time: 10 minutes
Cooking time: 18 minutes
 Servings: 6

Ingredients:
1¾ cups spelt flour
1¼ cup whole spelt
⅔ cup coconut sugar
2 teaspoons baking powder
½ teaspoon salt
3 tablespoons lemon zest
½ cup coconut oil
1 cup coconut cream
2 tablespoons almond milk
2 cups frozen raspberries
Directions
Preheat your oven to 425 degrees F.

Whisk dry ingredients in a stand mixer using whisk attachment.

Freeze the dry mixture for 10 minutes then place it back on the mixer.

Using the paddle attachment, stir in coconut oil, coconut cream, and almond milk then beat until smooth.

Fold in frozen raspberries and mix again, divide the dough into two parts.

Spread each part into a thick disk and cut each into 6 wedges of equal size.

Line a suitable baking sheet with parchment paper and place the wedges on the tray.

Bake for 18 minutes then serve.

Nutrition: Calories 119 Total Fat 14 g Saturated Fat 2 g Cholesterol 65 mg Sodium 269 mg Total Carbs 19 g Fiber 4 g Sugar 6 g Protein 5g

Veggie Breakfast Scramble

Preparation time: 10 minutes
Cooking time: 14 minutes
Servings: 06
Ingredients:

1 cup yellow onions, chopped
1 cup red bell peppers, diced
1½ cups zucchini, sliced
3 cups cauliflower florets
1 tablespoon garlic, minced
1 tablespoon tamari
2 tablespoons vegetable broth
2 tablespoons nutritional yeast
1 (15 ounce) can chickpeas, drained
2 cups baby spinach, chopped
Spice Mix:
1 teaspoon onion powder
1 teaspoon garlic powder
1 teaspoon dried minced onions
¾ teaspoon dried ground mustard powder
1 teaspoon dried thyme leaves
1 teaspoon smoked paprika
¼ teaspoon turmeric
¾ teaspoon salt
¼ teaspoon black pepper
Directions
In a suitable pan, add cooking oil and all the vegetables.
Cook while stirring for 7 minutes on medium heat.
Toss in the chickpeas and all the spices.
Continue sautéing for another 7 minutes.
Serve warm.
Nutrition: Calories 231 Fat 20.1 g Carbs 20 g

Chocolate PB Smoothie

Preparation time: 5 minutes
Cooking time: 0 minutes
Servings: 4
Ingredients
1 banana
¼ cup rolled oats, or 1 scoop plant protein powder
1 tablespoon flaxseed, or chia seeds
1 tablespoon unsweetened cocoa powder
1 tablespoon peanut butter, or almond or sunflower seed butter
1 tablespoon maple syrup (optional)
1 cup alfalfa sprouts, or spinach, chopped (optional)
½ cup non-dairy milk (optional)
1 cup water
Optional
1 teaspoon maca powder
1 teaspoon cocoa nibs
Directions
Purée everything in a blender until smooth, adding more water (or non-dairy milk) if needed.

Add bonus boosters, as desired. Purée until blended.
Nutrition: calories: 474; protein: 13g; total fat: 16g; carbohydrates: 79g; fiber: 18g

Orange French Toast

Preparation time: 15 minutes
Cooking time: 10 minutes
Servings: 4
Ingredients
3 very ripe bananas
1 cup unsweetened nondairy milk
Zest and juice of 1 orange
1 teaspoon ground cinnamon
¼ Teaspoon grated nutmeg
4 slices french bread
1 tablespoon coconut oil
Directions
In a blender, combine the bananas, almond milk, orange juice and zest, cinnamon, and nutmeg and blend until smooth. Pour the mixture into a 9-by-13-inch baking dish. Soak the bread in the mixture for 5 minutes on each side.

While the bread soaks, heat a griddle or sauté pan over medium-high heat. Melt the coconut oil in the pan and swirl to coat. Cook the bread slices until golden brown on both sides, about 5 minutes each. Serve immediately.

Oatmeal Raisin Breakfast Cookie

Preparation time: 5 minutes
Cooking time: 15 minutes
Servings: 2 cookies
Ingredients
½ Cup rolled oats
1 tablespoon whole-grain flour
½ Teaspoon baking powder
1 to 2 tablespoons brown sugar
½ Teaspoon pumpkin pie spice or ground cinnamon (optional)

¼ Cup unsweetened applesauce, plus more as needed

2 tablespoons raisins, dried cranberries, or vegan chocolate chips

Directions

In a medium bowl, stir together the oats, flour, baking powder, sugar, and pumpkin pie spice (if using). Stir in the applesauce until thoroughly combined. Add another 1 to 2 tablespoons of applesauce if the mixture looks too dry (this will depend on the type of oats used).

Shape the mixture into 2 cookies. Put them on a microwave-safe plate and heat on high power for 90 seconds. Alternatively, bake on a small tray in a 350°f oven or toaster oven for 15 minutes. Let cool slightly before eating.

Nutrition (2 cookies): calories: 175; protein: 74g; total fat: 2g; saturated fat:0g; carbohydrates: 39g; fiber: 4g

Berry Beetsicle Smoothie

Preparation time: 3 minutes
Cooking time: 0minutes
Servings: 1
Ingredients
½ Cup peeled and diced beets
½ Cup frozen raspberries
1 frozen banana
1 tablespoon maple syrup
1 cup unsweetened soy or almond milk
Directions
Combine all the Ingredients in a blender and blend until smooth.

Blueberry Oat Muffins

Preparation time: 10 minutes
Cooking time: 20 minutes
Servings: 12 mufins
Ingredients
2 tablespoons coconut oil or vegan margarine, melted, plus more for preparing the muffin tin
1 cup quick-cooking oats or instant oats
1 cup boiling water
½ Cup nondairy milk
¼ Cup ground flaxseed
1 teaspoon vanilla extract
1 teaspoon apple cider vinegar
1½ cups whole-grain flour
½ Cup brown sugar
2 teaspoons baking soda
Pinch salt
1 cup blueberries

Directions
Preheat the oven to 400°f.

Coat a muffin tin with coconut oil, line with paper muffin cups, or use a nonstick tin.

In a large bowl, combine the oats and boiling water. Stir so the oats soften. Add the coconut oil, milk, flaxseed, vanilla, and vinegar and stir to combine. Add the flour, sugar, baking soda, and salt. Stir until just combined. Gently fold in the blueberries. Scoop the muffin mixture into the prepared tin, about ⅓ cup for each muffin.

Bake for 20 to 25 minutes, until slightly browned on top and springy to the touch. Let cool for about 10 minutes. Run a dinner knife around the inside of each cup to loosen, then tilt the muffins on their sides in the muffin wells so air gets underneath. These keep in an airtight container in the refrigerator for up to 1 week or in the freezer indefinitely.

Nutrition (1muffin): calories: 174; protein: 5g; total fat: 3g; saturated fat:2g; carbohydrates: 33g; fiber: 4g

Quinoa Applesauce Muffins

Preparation time: 10 minutes
Cooking time: 15 minutes
Servings: 5
Ingredients
2 tablespoons coconut oil or margarine, melted, plus more for coating the muffin tin
¼ Cup ground flaxseed
½ Cup water
2 cups unsweetened applesauce
½ Cup brown sugar
1 teaspoon apple cider vinegar
2½ cups whole-grain flour
1½ cups cooked quinoa
2 teaspoons baking soda
Pinch salt
½ Cup dried cranberries or raisins

Directions

Preheat the oven to 400°f.

Coat a muffin tin with coconut oil, line with paper muffin cups, or use a nonstick tin. In a large bowl, stir together the flaxseed and water. Add the applesauce, sugar, coconut oil, and vinegar. Stir to combine. Add the flour, quinoa, baking soda, and salt, stirring until just combined. Gently fold in the cranberries without stirring too much. Scoop the muffin mixture into the prepared tin, about ⅓ cup for each muffin.

Bake for 15 to 20 minutes, until slightly browned on top and springy to the touch. Let cool for about 10 minutes. Run a dinner knife around the inside of each cup to loosen, then tilt the muffins on their sides in the muffin wells so air gets underneath. These keep in an airtight container in the refrigerator for up to 1 week or in the freezer indefinitely.

Per serving(1muffin): calories: 387; protein: 7g; total fat: 5g; saturated fat: 2g; carbohydrates: 57g; fiber: 8g

Pumpkin Pancakes

Preparation time: 15 minutes
Cooking time: 15 minutes
Servings: 4
Ingredients
2 cups unsweetened almond milk
1 teaspoon apple cider vinegar
2½ cups whole-wheat flour
2 tablespoons baking powder
½ Teaspoon baking soda
1 teaspoon sea salt
1 teaspoon pumpkin pie spice or ½ teaspoon ground -cinnamon plus ¼ teaspoon grated -nutmeg plus ¼ teaspoon ground allspice
½ Cup canned pumpkin purée
1 cup water
1 tablespoon coconut oil
Directions

In a small bowl, combine the almond milk and apple cider vinegar. Set aside.

In a bowl, whisk together the flour, baking powder, baking soda, salt, and pumpkin pie spice. In bowl, combine the almond milk mixture, pumpkin purée, and water, whisking to mix well. Mix the wet Ingredients to the dry Ingredients and fold together until the dry -Ingredients are just moistened.

In a nonstick pan or griddle over medium-high heat, melt the coconut oil and swirl to coat. Pour the batter into the pan ¼ cup at a time and cook

until the pancakes are browned, about 5 minutes per side. Serve immediately.

Green Breakfast Smoothie

Preparation time: 10 minutes
Cooking time: 0 minutes
Servings: 2
Ingredients
½ Banana, sliced
2 cups spinach or other greens, such as kale
1 cup sliced berries of your choosing, fresh or frozen
1 orange, peeled and cut into segments
1 cup unsweetened nondairy milk
1 cup ice
Directions

In a blender, combine all the Ingredients.

Starting with the blender on low speed, begin blending the smoothie, gradually increasing blender speed until smooth. Serve immediately.

Blueberry And Chia Smoothie

Preparation time: 10 minutes
Cooking time: 0 minutes
Servings: 2
Ingredients
2 tablespoons chia seeds
2 cups unsweetened nondairy milk
2 cups blueberries, fresh or frozen
2 tablespoons pure maple syrup or agave
2 tablespoons cocoa powder
Directions:

Soak the chia seeds in the almond milk for 5 minutes.

In a blender, combine the soaked chia seeds, almond milk, blueberries, maple syrup, and cocoa powder and blend until smooth. Serve immediately.

Warm Maple and Cinnamon Quinoa

Preparation time: 5 minutes
Cooking time: 15 minutes
Servings: 4
Ingredients
1 cup unsweetened nondairy milk
1 cup water
1 cup quinoa, rinsed
1 teaspoon cinnamon
¼ Cup chopped pecans or other nuts or seeds, such as chia, sunflower seeds, or almonds
2 tablespoons pure maple syrup or agave
Directions:

In a medium saucepan over medium-high heat, bring the almond milk, water, and quinoa to a boil. Lower the heat to medium-low and cover. Simmer until the liquid is mostly absorbed and the quinoa softens, about 15 minutes.

Turn off the heat and allow to sit, covered, for 5 minutes. Stir in the cinnamon, pecans, and syrup. Serve hot.

Warm Quinoa Breakfast Bowl

Preparation time: 5 minutes
Cooking time: 0 minutes
Servings: 4
Ingredients
3 cups freshly cooked quinoa
1⅓ cups unsweetened soy or almond milk
2 bananas, sliced
1 cup raspberries
1 cup blueberries
½ Cup chopped raw walnuts
¼ Cup maple syrup
Directions:
Divide the Ingredients among 4 bowls, starting with a base of ¾ cup quinoa, ⅓ cup milk, ½ banana, ¼ cup raspberries, ¼ cup blueberries, and 2 tablespoons walnuts.

Drizzle 1 tablespoon of maple syrup over the top of each bowl.

Banana Bread Rice Pudding

Preparation time: 5 minutes
Cooking time: 50 minutes
Servings: 4
Ingredients
1cup brown rice
1½ cups water
1½ cups nondairy milk
3 tablespoons sugar (omit if using a sweetened nondairy milk)
2 teaspoons pumpkin pie spice or ground cinnamon
2 bananas
3 tablespoons chopped walnuts or sunflower seeds (optional)
Directions
In a medium pot, combine the rice, water, milk, sugar, and pumpkin pie spice. Bring to a boil over high heat, turn the heat to low, and cover the pot. Simmer, stirring occasionally, until the rice is soft and the liquid is absorbed. White rice takes about 20 minutes; brown rice takes about 50 minutes.

Smash the bananas and stir them into the cooked rice. Serve topped with walnuts (if using). Leftovers will keep refrigerated in an airtight container for up to 5 days.

Nutrition: calories: 479; protein: 9g; total fat: 13g; saturated fat: 1g; carbohydrates: 86g; fiber: 7g

Apple and Cinnamon Oatmeal

Preparation time: 10 minutes
Cooking time:10 minutes
Servings: 2
Ingredients
1¼ cups apple cider
1 apple, peeled, cored, and chopped
⅔ Cup rolled oats
1 teaspoon ground cinnamon
1 tablespoon pure maple syrup or agave (optional)
Directions
In a medium saucepan, bring the apple cider to a boil over medium-high heat. Stir in the apple, oats, and cinnamon.

Bring the cereal to a boil and turn down heat to low. Simmer until the oatmeal thickens, 3 to 4 minutes. Spoon into two bowls and sweeten with maple syrup, if using. Serve hot.

Mango Key Lime Pie Smoothie

Preparation time: 5 minutes
Cooking time: 0 minutes
Servings: 1
Ingredients
¼ Avocado
1 cup baby spinach
½ Cup frozen mango chunks
1 cup unsweetened soy or almond milk
Juice of 1 lime (preferably a key lime).

1 tablespoon maple syrup
Directions
Combine all the Ingredients in a blender and blend until smooth. Enjoy immediately.

Breakfast Parfaits

Preparation time: 15 minutes
Cooking time: 0 minutes
Servings: 2
Ingredients
One 14-ounce can coconut milk, refrigerated overnight
1 cup granola
½ Cup walnuts
1 cup sliced strawberries or other seasonal berries
Directions
Pour off the canned coconut-milk liquid and retain the solids.
In two parfait glasses, layer the coconut-milk solids, granola, walnuts, and -strawberries. Serve immediately.

Sweet Potato And Kale Hash

Preparation time: 10 minutes
Cooking time: 15 minutes
Servings: 2
Ingredients
1 sweet potato
2 tablespoons olive oil
½ Onion, chopped
1 carrot, peeled and chopped
2 garlic cloves, minced
½ Teaspoon dried thyme
1 cup chopped kale
Sea salt
Freshly ground black pepper
Directions
Prick the sweet potato with a fork and microwave on high until soft, about 5 minutes. Remove from the microwave and cut into ¼-inch cubes.
In a large nonstick sauté pan, heat the olive oil over medium-high heat. Add the onion and carrot and cook until softened, about 5 minutes. Add the garlic and thyme and cook until the garlic is fragrant, about 30 seconds.
Add the sweet potatoes and cook until the potatoes begin to brown, about 7 -minutes. Add the kale and cook just until it wilts, 1 to 2 minutes. Season with salt and pepper. Serve immediately.

Delicious Oat Meal

Preparation time: 10 minutes
Cooking time: 6 hours
Servings: 4
Ingredients:
3 cups water
3 cups almond milk
1 and ½ cups steel oats
4 dates, pitted and chopped
1 teaspoon cinnamon, ground
2 tablespoons coconut sugar
½ Teaspoon ginger powder
A pinch of nutmeg, ground
A pinch of cloves, ground
1 teaspoon vanilla extract
Directions:
Put water and milk in your slow cooker and stir.
Add oats, dates, cinnamon, sugar, ginger, nutmeg, cloves and vanilla extract, stir, cover and cook on low for 6 hours.
Divide into bowls and serve for breakfast.
Enjoy!
Nutrition: calories 120, fat 1, fiber 2, carbs 3, protein 5

Breakfast Cherry Delight

Preparation time: 10 minutes
Cooking time: 8 hours and 10 minutes
Servings: 4
Ingredients:
2 cups almond milk
2 cups water
1 cup steel cut oats
2 tablespoons cocoa powder
1/3 cup cherries, pitted
¼ Cup maple syrup
½ Teaspoon almond extract
For the sauce:
2 tablespoons water
1 and ½ cups cherries, pitted and chopped
¼ Teaspoon almond extract
Directions:
Put the almond milk in your slow cooker.
Add 2 cups water, oats, cocoa powder, 1/3 cup cherries, maples syrup and ½ teaspoon almond extract.
Stir, cover and cook on low for 8 hours.
In a small pan, mix 2 tablespoons water with 1 and ½ cups cherries and ¼ teaspoon almond extract, stir well, bring to a simmer over medium heat and cook for 10 minutes until it thickens.

Divide oatmeal into breakfast bowls, top with the cherries sauce and serve.

Enjoy!

Nutrition: calories 150, fat 1, fiber 2, carbs 6, protein 5

Crazy Maple and Pear Breakfast

Preparation time: 10 minutes
Cooking time: 9 hours
Servings: 2
Ingredients:
1 pear, cored and chopped
½ Teaspoon maple extract
2 cups coconut milk
½ Cup steel cut oats
½ Teaspoon vanilla extract
1 tablespoon stevia
¼ Cup walnuts, chopped for serving
Cooking spray
Directions:

Spray your slow cooker with some cooking spray and add coconut milk.

Also, add maple extract, oats, pear, stevia and vanilla extract, stir, cover and cook on low for 9 hours.

Stir your oatmeal again, divide it into breakfast bowls and serve with chopped walnuts on top.

Enjoy!

Nutrition: calories 150, fat 3, fiber 2, carbs 6, protein 6

Hearty French Toast Bowls

Preparation time: 10 minutes
Cooking time: 5 hours
Servings: 4
Ingredients:
1 and ½ cups almond milk
1 cup coconut cream
1 tablespoon vanilla extract
½ Tablespoon cinnamon powder
2 tablespoons maple syrup
¼ Cup spenda
2 apples, cored and cubed
½ Cup cranberries, dried
1 pound vegan bread, cubed
Cooking spray
Directions:

Spray your slow cooker with some cooking spray and add the bread.

Also, add cranberries and apples and stir gently.

Add milk, coconut cream, maple syrup, vanilla extract, cinnamon powder and splenda.

Stir, cover and cook on low for 5 hours.

Divide into bowls and serve right away.

Enjoy!

Nutrition: calories 140, fat 2, fiber 3, carbs 6, protein 2

Entrées

Black Bean Dip

Preparation time: 1 hour and 30 minutes
Cooking time: 1 hour
Servings: 10
Ingredients:
2 15-ounce cans black beans, rinsed and drained
1 jalapeno pepper, seeded and minced
½ of a red bell pepper, seeded and diced
½ of a yellow bell pepper, seeded and diced
½ of s small red onion, diced
1 cup fresh cilantro, finely chopped
Zest of 1 lime
Juice of 1 lime
1 10-ounce can Ro*tel, drained
½ teaspoon Kosher salt
¼ teaspoon ground black pepper
Directions:
In a large bowl, combine the garlic, green onions, beans, jalapeno, red and yellow bell pepper, onion, cilantro and mix together well.

Add the lime zest and juice, Ro-tel, salt and pepper and mix. Adjust seasoning to your own taste.

Refrigerate for at one hour, minimum, before serving, so the flavors have time to blend. Serve with wheat tortilla slices that have been crisped in the oven or with wheat or sesame crackers.

Cauliflower Popcorn

Preparation time: 1 day and 1 hour
Cooking time: 1 day
Servings: 2
Ingredients:
¼ cup sun-dried tomatoes
¾ cup dates
2 heads cauliflower
½ cup water
2 tablespoons raw tahini
1 tablespoon apple cider vinegar
2 teaspoons onion powder
2 teaspoons garlic powder
1 teaspoon ground cayenne pepper
2 tablespoons nutritional yeast (optional)
Directions:
Cover the sun-dried tomatoes warm water and let them soak for an hour.

If the dates are not soft and fresh, soak them in warm water for an hour in another bowl.

Cut the cauliflower in very small, bite-sized pieces then set aside.

Put the drained tomatoes and dates in a blender along with the water, tahini, apple cider vinegar, onion powder, garlic powder, cayenne pepper, nutritional yeast and turmeric. Blend into a thick, smooth consistency.

Pour this mixture into the bowl, atop the cauliflower and mix so that all the pieces are coated.

Place the cauliflower in the dehydrator and spread it out to make a single layer. Sprinkle with a little sea salt and set for 115 degrees, Fahrenheit for 12 to 24 hours or until it becomes exactly as crunchy as you like it. I let mine go for 15 to 16 hours, but the time will vary based on your taste preference as well as the ambient humidity.

Store in an airtight container until serving.

Cinnamon Apple Chips with Dip

Preparation time: 3 hours and 30 minutes
Cooking time: 3 hours
Servings: 2
Ingredients:
1 cup raw cashews
2 apples, thinly sliced
1 lemon
1½ cups water, divided
Cinnamon plus more to dust the chips
Another medium cored apple quartered
1 tablespoon honey or agave
1 teaspoon cinnamon
¼ teaspoon sea salt
Directions:
Place the cashews in a bowl of warm water, deep enough to cover them and let them soak overnight.

Preheat the oven to 200 degrees, Fahrenheit. Line two baking sheets with parchment paper.

Juice the lemon into a large glass bowl and add two cups of the water. Place the sliced apples in the water as you cut them and when done, swish them around and drain.

Spread the apple slices across the baking sheet in a single layer and sprinkle with a little cinnamon. Bake for 90 minutes.

Remove the slices from the oven and flip each of them over. Put them back in the oven and bake for another 90 minutes, or until they are crisp. Remember, they will get crisper as they cool.

While the apple slices are cooking, drain the cashews and put them in a blender, along with the quartered apple, the honey, a teaspoon of cinnamon and a half cup of the remaining water. Process until thick and creamy. I like to refrigerate my dip for about an hour to chill, before serve alongside the room temperature apple slices.

Crunchy Asparagus Spears

Preparation time: 25 minutes
Cooking time: 25 minutes
Servings: 4
Ingredients:
1 bunch asparagus spears (about 12 spears)
¼ cup nutritional yeast
2 tablespoons hemp seeds
1 teaspoon garlic powder
¼ teaspoon paprika (or more if you like paprika)
⅛ teaspoon ground pepper
¼ cup whole-wheat breadcrumbs
Juice of ½ lemon
Directions:
Preheat the oven to 350 degrees, Fahrenheit. Line a baking sheet with parchment paper.

Wash the asparagus, snapping off the white part at the bottom. Save it for making vegetable stock.

Mix together the nutritional yeast, hemp seed, garlic powder, paprika, pepper and breadcrumbs.

Place asparagus spears on the baking sheets giving them a little room in between and sprinkle with the mixture in the bowl.

Bake for up to 25 minutes, until crispy. Serve with lemon juice if desired.

Cucumber Bites with Chive and Sunflower Seeds

Preparation time: 5 minutes
Cooking time: 5 minutes
Servings: 2
Ingredients:
1 cup raw sunflower seed
½ teaspoon salt
½ cup chopped fresh chives
1 clove garlic, chopped
2 tablespoons red onion, minced
2 tablespoons lemon juice
½ cup water (might need more or less)
4 large cucumbers
Directions:
Place the sunflower seeds and salt in the food processor and process to a fine powder. It will take only about 10 seconds.

Add the chives, garlic, onion, lemon juice and water and process until creamy, scraping down the sides frequently. The mixture should be very creamy; if not, add a little more water.

Cut the cucumbers into 1½-inch coin-like pieces.

Spread a spoonful of the sunflower mixture on top and set on a platter. Sprinkle more chopped chives on top and refrigerate until ready to serve.

Garlicky Kale Chips

Preparation time: 1 hour and 30 min
Cooking time: 1 hour
Servings: 2
Ingredients:
4 cloves garlic
1 cup olive oil
8 to 10 cups fresh kale, chopped
1 tablespoon of garlic-flavored olive oil

½ teaspoon garlic salt
½ teaspoon pepper
1 pinch red pepper flakes (optional)
Directions:
Peel and crush the garlic clove and place it in a small jar with a lid. Pour the olive oil over the top, cover tightly and shake. This will keep in the refrigerator for several days. When you're ready to use it, strain out the garlic and retain the oil.

Preheat the oven to 175 degrees, Fahrenheit.

Spread out the kale on a baking sheet and drizzle with the olive oil. Sprinkle with garlic salt, pepper and red pepper flakes.

Bake for an hour, remove from the oven and let the chips cool.

Store in an airtight container if you don't plan to eat them right away.

Hummus-stuffed Baby Potatoes

Preparation time: 30 minutes
Cooking time: 30 minutes
Servings: 2
Ingredients:
12 small red potatoes, walnut-sized or slightly larger
Hummus
2 green onions, thinly sliced
¼ teaspoon paprika, for garnish
Directions:
Place two to three inches of water in a saucepan, set a steamer inside and bring the water to a boil.

Place the whole potatoes in the steamer basket and steam for about 20 minutes or until soft. Keep the pan from boiling dry by adding additional hot water as needed.

Dump the potatoes into a colander and run cold water over them until they can be handled.

Cut each potato open and scoop out most of the pulp, leaving the skin and a thin layer of potato intact.

Mix the hummus with most of the green onions (keep enough for garnish) and spoon a little into the area where the potato has been scooped out.

Sprinkle each filled potato half with paprika and serve.

Homemade Trail Mix

Preparation time: 20 minutes
Cooking time: 20 minutes
Servings: 2
Ingredients:
½ cup uncooked old-fashioned oatmeal
½ cup chopped dates
2 cups whole grain cereal
¼ cup raisins
¼ cup almonds
¼ cup walnuts
Directions:
Mix all the ingredients in a large bowl.
Place in an airtight container until ready to use.

Oven Baked Sesame Fries

Preparation time: 30 minutes
   Cooking time: 30 minutes
   Servings: 4
   Ingredients:
   1 pound Yukon Gold potatoes, skins on and
cut into wedges
   2 tablespoons sesame seeds
   1 tablespoon potato starch
   1 tablespoon sesame oil
   Salt to taste
   Black pepper to taste
   Directions:
   Preheat the oven to 425 degrees, Fahrenheit
and cover a baking sheet or two with parchment
paper.

Cut the potatoes and place in a large bowl.
Add the sesame seeds, potato starch, sesame oil, salt and pepper.
Toss with your hands and make sure all the wedges are coated. Add more sesame seeds or oil if needed.
Spread the potato wedges on the baking sheets with some room between each wedge.
Bake for 15 minutes, flip the wedges over and then return them to the oven for 10 to 15 more minutes, until they look golden and crispy.

Pumpkin Orange Spice Hummus

Preparation time: 30 minutes
Cooking time: 30 minutes
Servings: 3
Ingredients:
1 cup canned, unsweetened pumpkin puree
1 16-ounce can garbanzo beans, rinsed and drained
1 tablespoon apple cider vinegar
1 tablespoon maple syrup
¼ cup tahini
1 tablespoon fresh orange juice
½ teaspoon orange zest and additional zest for garnish
⅛ teaspoon ground cinnamon
⅛ teaspoon ground ginger
⅛ teaspoon ground nutmeg
¼ teaspoon salt
Directions:
Pour the pumpkin puree and garbanzo beans into a food processor and pulse to break up.
Add the vinegar, syrup, tahini, orange juice and orange zest pulse a few times.
Add the cinnamon, ginger, nutmeg and salt and process until smooth and creamy.
Serve in a bowl sprinkled with more orange zest with wheat crackers alongside.

Quinoa Trail Mix Cups

Preparation time: 30 minutes
Cooking time: 30 minutes
Servings: 16
Ingredients:
2 tablespoons ground flaxseed
⅓ cup unsweetened soy milk
1 cup old-fashioned rolled oats
1 cup cooked and cooled quinoa
¼ cup brown sugar
1 teaspoon ground cinnamon
¼ teaspoon salt
¼ cup pumpkin or sunflower seeds
¼ cup shredded coconut
½ cup almonds
½ cup raisins or dried cherries/cranberries
Directions:
Whisk the flaxseed and milk together in a small bowl and set aside for 10 minutes so the seed can absorb the milk.

Preheat the oven to 350 degrees, Fahrenheit and coat a muffin tin with coconut oil.

In a large bowl, mix the oats, quinoa, brown sugar, cinnamon, salt, pumpkin seeds, coconut, almonds and raisins.

Stir in the flaxseed and milk mixture and combine thoroughly.

Place two heaping teaspoons of the trail mix mixture in each muffin cup. When done, wet your fingers and press down on each muffin cup to compact the trail mix.

Bake for 12 minutes.

Cool completely before removing and each little cup will fall out. Store in an airtight container.

Lemon & Ginger Kale Chips

Preparation Time: 30 Minutes
Cooking Time: 10 Minutes
Servings: 5
Ingredients:
Ginger (1 t.)
Salt (to Taste)
Lemon Zest (1 t.)
Olive Oil (1 T.)
Kale (7 Oz.)
Directions:
Before you begin cooking this delicious snack, you'll want to prepare the oven to 300. As this warms up, go ahead and line your baking sheet with parchment paper.

Next, you are going to want to place your kale into a bowl and toss with the olive oil, lemon zest, ginger, and the salt. Give everything a good toss to spread the seasonings over all of the kale.

When the kale is set, spread it out evenly onto your baking sheet and pop into the oven for ten minutes. By the end of this time, the edges of the leaves should look dry.

If the kale is cooked to your liking, remove from the oven and allow to cool completely before serving.

Nutrition: Calories: 45 Proteins: 1g Carbs: 4g Fats: 3g

Chocolate Energy Snack Bar

Preparation Time: 5 Minutes
Cooking Time: 0 Minutes
Servings: 4
Ingredients:
Flax Seeds (1 T.)
Chia Seeds (1 T.)
Agave Nectar (2 T.)
Almonds (1 C.)
Dried Cranberries (1 C.)
Dates (1 C.)
Directions:

When you need a snack that is easy to grab when you are on the go, this is the perfect recipe. You are going to start out by pulsing the almonds and dates in a food processor. Once they are chopped fine, add in the seeds, agave, and cranberries. At this point, pulse until everything is combined.

Next, you will want to add the batter into a lined pan and press everything down into the bottom.

Finally, pop the dish into the fridge for two hours, cut into squares, and your bars are ready!

Nutrition: Calories: 400 Proteins: 10g Carbs: 55g Fats: 20g

Hazelnut & Maple Chia Crunch

Preparation Time: 30 Minutes

Cooking Time: 5 Minutes
Servings: 2
Ingredients:
Chia Seeds (.25 C.)
Olive Oil (1 t.)
Maple Syrup (.50 C.)
Hazelnuts (1.25 C.)
Salt (to Taste)
Directions:

To begin this recipe, start by heating a pan over medium heat. Once warm, place the olive oil and maple in and bring to a boil.

Once boiling, stir in your hazelnuts and cook on high for a minute or two. After this time passes, add in the chia seeds and salt and cook for another three minutes.

Now, turn the heat down to low and begin crushing the hazelnuts in the pan before pouring onto a lined cookie sheet. At this point, try to spread the mixture evenly across the pan and then place it in the freezer for 15 minutes.

Once the mixture has completely cooled, chop the ingredients into clusters and enjoy.

Nutrition: Calories: 330 Proteins: 3g Carbs: 60g Fats: 11g

Roasted Cauliflower

Preparation Time: 30 Minutes
Cooking Time: 20 Minutes
Servings: 4
Ingredients:
Olive Oil (1 T.)
Cauliflower (1, Chopped)
Salt (to Taste)
Smoked Paprika (2 t.)
Parsley (2 T.)
Directions:

If you like to snack, it is better to have healthier options at hand. You'll want to start this recipe off by prepping your oven to 450.

As this warms up, place the cauliflower florets into a large mixing bowl and toss with the olive oil, salt, and smoked paprika. Once this is complete, lay it across a baking sheet and pop it into the oven for 20 minutes.

When the cauliflower is cooked to your liking, remove from the oven, top with parsley, and you are all set.

Nutrition: Calories: 70 Proteins: 3g Carbs: 8g Fats: 5g

Apple Cinnamon Crisps

Preparation Time: 2 Hours
Cooking Time: 2 Hours
Servings: 2
Ingredients:
Cinnamon (1 t.)
Apple (1, Sliced)
Directions:

This recipe is simple and delicious! You can start off by turning the oven to 200. As this warms up, you'll want to prep a baking sheet with some parchment paper.

With the baking sheet set, layout your apple slices across it evenly and sprinkle with the cinnamon. Once this is done, pop the dish into the oven for two hours.

Remove from oven, allow to cool, and enjoy.

Nutrition: Calories: 50 Proteins: 5g Carbs: 14g Fats: 1g

Salted Carrot Fries

Preparation Time: 30 Minutes
Cooking Time: 20 Minutes
Servings: 4
Ingredients:
Olive Oil (2 T.)
Salt (to taste)
Carrots (6)
Directions:

Begin by prepping your oven to 425. While this warms up, line a baking sheet with parchment paper and set to the side.

Next, you will want to take your carrots and carefully cut them into smaller sections, resembling fries.

Once the carrots are cut, you will want to toss them in a bowl with the salt and olive oil. As you do this, make sure the carrots are evenly coated.

Finally, pop the dish into the oven for twenty minutes. By the end, the carrots should be slightly browned and cooked through. If it is cooked to your liking, allow to cool and then enjoy.

Nutrition: Calories: 100 Proteins: 1g

Zesty Orange Muffins

Preparation Time: 40 Minutes
Cooking Time: 20 Minutes
Servings: 11
Ingredients:
Chopped Hazelnuts (3 T.)
Orange Juice (1 C.)
Olive Oil (.50 C.)
Baking Powder (2 t.)
Brown Sugar (.75 C.)
Flour (2 C.)
Baking Soda (1 Pinch)
Salt (to Taste)
Orange Zest (2 T.)
Directions:

Muffins are the perfect snack to grab and go when you need to leave the house quickly. Start off by prepping the oven to 350.

As this warms up, take out your mixing bowl and combine the hazelnuts, salt, baking soda, baking powder, sugar, and flour. Once these are mixed together well, add in the olive oil and orange juice.

With your mixture made, evenly pour into lined muffin tins and then pop it into the oven for 20 minutes.

By the end, the muffins should be cooked through and golden at the top. If they look done, remove from the oven, and your snack is ready to go.

Nutrition: Calories: 220 Proteins: 3g Carbs: 30g Fats: 10g

Chocolate Tahini Balls

Preparation Time: 10 Minutes
Cooking Time: 0 Minutes
Servings: 8
Ingredients:
Sesame Seeds (2 T.)
Tahini (2 T.)
Cacao Nibs (2 T.)
Unsweetened Cocoa Powder (2 T.)
Old-fashioned Rolled Oats (.25 C.)
Medjool Dates (4)
Rock Salt (1 Pinch)
Directions:
For this quick snack, start off by placing all of the ingredients above into a blender and blend until you get a dough-like texture.

Next, take the dough and mold it into 8 balls.

Place the balls in the fridge, allow to firm up for 20 minutes, and then they will be set.

Nutrition: Calories: 70 Proteins: 2g Carbs: 9g Fats: 4g

Coconut Watercress Soup

Preparation time: 10 minutes

Cooking time: 20 minutes
Servings: 4
 Ingredients:
1 teaspoon coconut oil
1 onion, diced
¾ cup coconut milk
Directions:
Preparing the ingredients.

Melt the coconut oil in a large pot over medium-high heat. Add the onion and cook until soft, about 5 minutes, then add the peas and the water. Bring to a boil, then lower the heat and add the watercress, mint, salt, and pepper.

Cover and simmer for 5 minutes. Stir in the coconut milk, and purée the soup until smooth in a blender or with an immersion blender.

Try this soup with any other fresh, leafy green—anything from spinach to collard greens to arugula to swiss chard.

Nutrition: calories: 178; protein: 6g; total fat: 10g; carbohydrates: 18g; fiber: 5g

Roasted Red Pepper and Butternut Squash Soup

Preparation time: 10 minutes
Cooking time: 45 minutes
Servings: 6
 Ingredients:
1 small butternut squash
1 tablespoon olive oil
1 teaspoon sea salt
2 red bell peppers
1 yellow onion
1 head garlic
2 cups water, or vegetable broth
Zest and juice of 1 lime
1 to 2 tablespoons tahini
Pinch cayenne pepper
½ teaspoon ground coriander
½ teaspoon ground cumin
Toasted squash seeds (optional)
Directions:
Preparing the ingredients.
Preheat the oven to 350°f.

Prepare the squash for roasting by cutting it in half lengthwise, scooping out the seeds, and poking some holes in the flesh with a fork. Reserve the seeds if desired.

Rub a small amount of oil over the flesh and skin, then rub with a bit of sea salt and put the halves skin-side down in a large baking dish. Put it in the oven while you prepare the rest of the vegetables.

Prepare the peppers the exact same way, except they do not need to be poked.

Slice the onion in half and rub oil on the exposed faces. Slice the top off the head of garlic and rub oil on the exposed flesh.

After the squash has cooked for 20 minutes, add the peppers, onion, and garlic, and roast for another 20 minutes. Optionally, you can toast the squash seeds by putting them in the oven in a separate baking dish 10 to 15 minutes before the vegetables are finished.

Keep a close eye on them. When the vegetables are cooked, take them out and let them cool before handling them. The squash will be very soft when poked with a fork.

Scoop the flesh out of the squash skin into a large pot (if you have an immersion blender) or into a blender.

Chop the pepper roughly, remove the onion skin and chop the onion roughly, and squeeze the garlic cloves out of the head, all into the pot or blender. Add the water, the lime zest and juice, and the tahini. Purée the soup, adding more water if you like, to your desired consistency. Season with the salt, cayenne, coriander, and cumin. Serve garnished with toasted squash seeds (if using).

Nutrition: calories: 156; protein: 4g; total fat: 7g; saturated fat: 11g; carbohydrates: 22g; fiber: 5g

Tomato Pumpkin Soup

Preparation time: 25 minutes
Cooking time: 15 minutes
Servings: 4
Ingredients:
2 cups pumpkin, diced
1/2 cup tomato, chopped
1/2 cup onion, chopped
1 1/2 tsp curry powder
1/2 tsp paprika
2 cups vegetable stock
1 tsp olive oil
1/2 tsp garlic, minced
Directions:
In a saucepan, add oil, garlic, and onion and sauté for 3 minutes over medium heat.

Add remaining ingredients into the saucepan and bring to boil.

Reduce heat and cover and simmer for 10 minutes.

Puree the soup using a blender until smooth.
Stir well and serve warm.

Nutrition: calories 70; fat 2.7 g; carbohydrates 13.8 g; sugar 6.3 g; protein 1.9 g; cholesterol 0 mg

Cauliflower Spinach Soup

Preparation time: 45 minutes
Cooking time: 25 minutes
Servings: 5
Ingredients:
1/2 cup unsweetened coconut milk
5 oz fresh spinach, chopped
5 watercress, chopped
8 cups vegetable stock
1 lb cauliflower, chopped
Salt
Directions:
Add stock and cauliflower in a large saucepan and bring to boil over medium heat for 15 minutes.

Add spinach and watercress and cook for another 10 minutes.

Remove from heat and puree the soup using a blender until smooth.

Add coconut milk and stir well. Season with salt.

Stir well and serve hot.

Nutrition: calories 153; fat 8.3 g; carbohydrates 8.7 g; sugar 4.3 g; protein 11.9 g; cholesterol 0 mg

Avocado Mint Soup

Preparation time: 10 minutes
Cooking time: 10 minutes
Servings: 2
Ingredients:
1 medium avocado, peeled, pitted, and cut into pieces
1 cup coconut milk
2 romaine lettuce leaves
20 fresh mint leaves
1 tbsp fresh lime juice
1/8 tsp salt

Directions:

Add all ingredients into the blender and blend until smooth. Soup should be thick not as a puree.

Pour into the serving bowls and place in the refrigerator for 10 minutes.

Stir well and serve chilled.

Nutrition: calories 268; fat 25.6 g; carbohydrates 10.2 g; sugar 0.6 g; protein 2.7 g; cholesterol 0 mg

Creamy Squash Soup

Preparation time: 35 minutes
Cooking time: 22 minutes
Servings: 8
Ingredients:
3 cups butternut squash, chopped
1 ½ cups unsweetened coconut milk
1 tbsp coconut oil
1 tsp dried onion flakes
1 tbsp curry powder
4 cups water
1 garlic clove
1 tsp kosher salt
Directions:

Add squash, coconut oil, onion flakes, curry powder, water, garlic, and salt into a large saucepan. Bring to boil over high heat.

Turn heat to medium and simmer for 20 minutes.

Puree the soup using a blender until smooth. Return soup to the saucepan and stir in coconut milk and cook for 2 minutes.

Stir well and serve hot.

Nutrition: calories 146; fat 12.6 g; carbohydrates 9.4 g; sugar 2.8 g; protein 1.7 g; cholesterol 0 mg

Cucumber Edamame Salad

Preparation time: 5 minutes
Cooking time: 8 minutes
Servings: 2
 Ingredients:
3 tbsp. Avocado oil
1 cup cucumber, sliced into thin rounds
½ cup fresh sugar snap peas, sliced or whole
½ cup fresh edamame
¼ cup radish, sliced
1 large avocado, peeled, pitted, sliced
1 nori sheet, crumbled
2 tsp. Roasted sesame seeds
1 tsp. Salt
Directions:

Bring a medium-sized pot filled halfway with water to a boil over medium-high heat.

Add the sugar snaps and cook them for about 2 minutes.

Take the pot off the heat, drain the excess water, transfer the sugar snaps to a medium-sized bowl and set aside for now.

Fill the pot with water again, add the teaspoon of salt and bring to a boil over medium-high heat.

Add the edamame to the pot and let them cook for about 6 minutes.

Take the pot off the heat, drain the excess water, transfer the soybeans to the bowl with sugar snaps and let them cool down for about 5 minutes.

Combine all ingredients, except the nori crumbs and roasted sesame seeds, in a medium-sized bowl.

Carefully stir, using a spoon, until all ingredients are evenly coated in oil.

Top the salad with the nori crumbs and roasted sesame seeds.

Transfer the bowl to the fridge and allow the salad to cool for at least 30 minutes.

Serve chilled and enjoy!

Nutrition: Calories 409 Carbohydrates 7.1 g Fats 38.25 g Protein 7.6 g

Best Broccoli Salad

Preparation time: 15 minutes
Chilling time: 1 hour
Servings: 8
Ingredients:
8 cups diced broccoli
¼ cup sunflower seeds
3 tablespoons apple cider vinegar
½ cup dried cranberries
1/3 cup cubed onion
1 cup mayonnaise
½ cup bacon bits
2 tablespoons sugar
½ teaspoon salt and ground black pepper
Directions:
In a bowl, mix vinegar, salt, pepper, mayonnaise, and sugar. Mix it well. In another bowl, mix all the remaining ingredients and pour the prepared mayonnaise dressing and mix it well. Before serving to refrigerate it for at least an hour.
Nutrition: Carbohydrates 17g, protein 6g, fats 26g, calories 317

Rainbow Orzo Salad

Preparation time: 10 minutes
Cooking time: 20 minutes
Servings: 1
Ingredients:
1 chopped onion
25g grated feta cheese
2 sliced bell peppers
1 tablespoon olive oil
6 sliced tomatoes
2 tablespoons chopped basil
25g orzo pasta
Directions:
Preheat the oven at 350f temperature. Prepare a baking sheet and place the onion and bell peppers and drizzle half olive oil. Bake it for around 15 minutes. Add tomatoes on it and bake for an additional 5 minutes. Meanwhile, cook the orzo according to the given directions on the pack and cool it. Now toss it with the baked vegetables and top it with cheese, basil and remaining oil and serve it.
Nutrition: Carbohydrates 52g, protein 13g, fats 18g, calories 422, sugar 30g.

Broccoli Pasta Salad

Preparation time: 15 minutes
Chilling time: 30 minutes
Servings: 12
Ingredients:
1-pound cooked pasta
2 diced broccoli florets
1 chopped onion
1 cup grated cheese
12 ounce cooked and finely chopped bacon
¾ teaspoon salt
¾ teaspoon ground black pepper
1 cup mayonnaise
Directions:
Take a bowl and mix all the ingredients until all of them combined well. Cover it with the plastic wrap and place it in the refrigerator for at least 30 minutes and serve it. You can keep it in the refrigerator for 3 days.
Nutrition: Carbohydrates 36g, protein 14g, fats 29g, calories 461.

Eggplant & Roasted Tomato Farro Salad

Preparation time: 1 hour
Cooking time: 1 hour 30 minutes
Servings: 3
Ingredients:
4 small eggplants
1 ½ cups chopped cherry tomatoes
¾ cup uncooked faro
1 tablespoon olive oil
1 minced garlic clove
½ cup rinsed and drained chickpeas
1 tablespoon basil
1 tablespoon arugula
½ teaspoon salt and ground black pepper
1 tablespoon vinegar
½ cup toasted pine nuts
Directions:
Preheat the oven at 300f temperature and prepare a baking sheet. Place cherry tomatoes on the baking liner and drizzle olive oil, salt, and black pepper on it and bake it for 30 to 35 minutes. Cook the faro in the salted water for 30 to 40 minutes. Slice the eggplant and salt it and

leave it for 30 minutes. After that, rinse it with water and dry it kitchen towel. Now peeled and sliced the eggplants. Now place these slices on the baking liner and season it with salt, pepper and olive oil. Bake it for 15 to 20 minutes in the preheated oven at the 450f temperature. Flip the sides of eggplant and bake it for an additional 15 to 20 minutes. Bake the pine nuts for 5 minutes and sauté the garlic. Now mix all the ingredients in a bowl and serve it.

Nutrition: Carbohydrates 37g, protein 9g, fats 25g, calories 399.

Garden Patch Sandwiches on Multigrain Bread

Preparation time: 15 minutes
Cooking time: 0 minutes
Servings: 4 sandwiches
Ingredients:
1pound extra-firm tofu, drained and patted dry
1 medium red bell pepper, finely chopped
1 celery rib, finely chopped
3 green onions, minced
1/4 cup shelled sunflower seeds
1/2 cup vegan mayonnaise, homemade or store-bought
1/2 teaspoon salt
1/2 teaspoon celery salt
1/4 teaspoon freshly ground black pepper
8 slices whole grain bread
4 (1/4-inch) slices ripe tomato
4 lettuce leaves
Directions:
Crumble the tofu and place it in a large bowl. Add the bell pepper, celery, green onions, and sunflower seeds. Stir in the mayonnaise, salt, celery salt, and pepper and mix until well combined.

Toast the bread, if desired. Spread the mixture evenly onto 4 slices of the bread. Top each with a tomato slice, lettuce leaf, and the remaining bread. Cut the sandwiches diagonally in half and serve.

Garden Salad Wraps

Preparation time: 15 minutes
Cooking time: 10 minutes
Servings: 4 wraps
Ingredients:
6 tablespoons olive oil
1-pound extra-firm tofu, drained, patted dry, and cut into 1/2-inch strips
1 tablespoon soy sauce
1/4 cup apple cider vinegar
1 teaspoon yellow or spicy brown mustard
1/2 teaspoon salt
1/4 teaspoon freshly ground black pepper
3 cups shredded romaine lettuce
3 ripe roma tomatoes, finely chopped
1 large carrot, shredded
1 medium english cucumber, peeled and chopped
1/3 cup minced red onion
1/4 cup sliced pitted green olives
4 (10-inch) whole-grain flour tortillas or lavash flatbread

Directions:
In a large skillet, heat 2 tablespoons of the oil over medium heat. Add the tofu and cook until golden brown, about 10 minutes. Sprinkle with soy sauce and set aside to cool.

In a small bowl, combine the vinegar, mustard, salt, and pepper with the remaining 4 tablespoons oil, stirring to blend well. Set aside.

In a large bowl, combine the lettuce, tomatoes, carrot, cucumber, onion, and olives. Pour on the dressing and toss to coat.

To assemble wraps, place 1 tortilla on a work surface and spread with about one-quarter of the salad. Place a few strips of tofu on the tortilla and roll up tightly. Slice in half

Marinated Mushroom Wraps

Preparation time: 15 minutes
Cooking time: 0 minutes
Servings: 2 wraps
Ingredients:
3 tablespoons soy sauce
3 tablespoons fresh lemon juice
1½ tablespoons toasted sesame oil
2 portobello mushroom caps, cut into ¼-inch strips
1 ripe hass avocado, pitted and peeled
2 cups fresh baby spinach leaves
1 medium red bell pepper, cut into ¼-inch strips
1 ripe tomato, chopped
Salt and freshly ground black pepper
Directions:
In a medium bowl, combine the soy sauce, 2 tablespoons of the lemon juice, and the oil. Add the portobello strips, toss to combine, and marinate for 1 hour or overnight. Drain the mushrooms and set aside.

Mash the avocado with the remaining 1 tablespoon of lemon juice.

To assemble wraps, place 1 tortilla on a work surface and spread with some of the mashed avocado. Top with a layer of baby spinach leaves. In the lower third of each tortilla, arrange strips of the soaked mushrooms and some of the bell pepper strips. Sprinkle with the tomato and salt and black pepper to taste. Roll up tightly and cut in half diagonally. Repeat with the remaining ingredients and serve.

Tamari Toasted Almonds

Preparation time: 2 minutes
Cooking time: 8 minutes
Servings: ½ cup
Ingredients:
½ cup raw almonds, or sunflower seeds
2 tablespoons tamari, or soy sauce
1 teaspoon toasted sesame oil
Directions:
Preparing the ingredients.

Heat a dry skillet to medium-high heat, then add the almonds, stirring very frequently to keep them from burning. Once the almonds are toasted, 7 to 8 minutes for almonds, or 3 to 4 minutes for sunflower seeds, pour the tamari and sesame oil into the hot skillet and stir to coat.

You can turn off the heat, and as the almonds cool the tamari mixture will stick to and dry on the nuts.

Nutrition: calories: 89; total fat: 8g; carbs: 3g; fiber: 2g; protein: 4g

Nourishing Whole-Grain Porridge

Preparation time: 2 hours and 10 minutes
Cooking time: 2 hours
Servings: 4
Ingredients:
3/4 cup of steel-cut oats, rinsed and soaked overnight
3/4 cup of whole barley, rinsed and soaked overnight
1/2 cup of cornmeal
1 teaspoon of salt
3 tablespoons of brown sugar
1 cinnamon stick, about 3 inches long
1 teaspoon of vanilla extract, unsweetened
4 1/2 cups of water
Directions:
Using a 6-quarts slow cooker, place all the ingredients and stir properly.

Cover it with the lid, plug in the slow cooker and let it cook for 2 hours or until grains get soft, while stirring halfway through.

Serve the porridge with fruits.
Nutrition: Calories: 129 Cal, Carbohydrates:22g, Protein:5g, Fats:2g, Fiber:4g.

Pungent Mushroom Barley Risotto

Preparation time: 3 hours and 30 minutes
Cooking time: 3 hours and 9 minutes
Servings: 4
Ingredients:
1 1/2 cups of hulled barley, rinsed and soaked overnight
8 ounces of carrots, peeled and chopped
1 pound of mushrooms, sliced
1 large white onion, peeled and chopped
3/4 teaspoon of salt
1/2 teaspoon of ground black pepper
4 sprigs thyme
1/4 cup of chopped parsley

2/3 cup of grated vegan Parmesan cheese
1 tablespoon of apple cider vinegar
2 tablespoons of olive oil
1 1/2 cups of vegetable broth
Directions:

Place a large non-stick skillet pan over a medium-high heat, add the oil and let it heat until it gets hot.

Add the onion along with 1/4 teaspoon of each the salt and black pepper.

Cook it for 5 minutes or until it turns golden brown.

Then add the mushrooms and continue cooking for 2 minutes.

Add the barley, thyme and cook for another 2 minutes.

Transfer this mixture to a 6-quarts slow cooker and add the carrots, 1/4 teaspoon of salt, and the vegetable broth.

Stir properly and cover it with the lid.

Plug in the slow cooker, let it cook for 3 hours at the high heat setting or until the grains absorb all the cooking liquid and the vegetables get soft.

Remove the thyme sprigs, pour in the remaining ingredients except for parsley and stir properly.

Pour in the warm water and stir properly until the risotto reaches your desired state.

Add the seasoning, then garnish it with parsley and serve.

Nutrition: Calories:321 Cal, Carbohydrates:48g, Protein:12g, Fats:10g, Fiber:11g.

Grilled Halloumi Broccoli Salad

Preparation time: 15 mins
Cooking time: 15 mins.
Ingredient: Fresh Salad
Halloumi Cheese (about 2/3 of a packet)
Half an Avocado
Baby Broccoli
Quinoa (half a cup)
Olive Oil (dressing).
Directions:

The first thing to do is to prepare your salad. Wash and dry it well. Once the halloumi is ready, you're going to want to eat it straight away as it tends to get very rubbery as it cools off so preparing everything else beforehand makes everything easier. Prepare half an avocado by slicing it into small cubes (it'll add creaminess to your salad which is why I tend to only use olive oil as my dressing).

In a pot, add some water to boil (with a pinch of salt) for the baby broccoli. I like mine fairly crunchy so 2-3 minutes was enough. Once your salad and avocado are done and your broccoli is cooking, start with your quinoa. Put half a cup of quinoa into a small pot, add about one cup of water and leave to boil (salt isn't necessary here because of the saltiness of the halloumi cheese) on a medium flame.

As your broccoli is cooking, prepare your grill pan for the halloumi cheese. On a medium flame, add a few drops of olive oil and leave it to heat up. Slice the halloumi into about centimetre thick pieces, then add to the grill pan. Your broccoli should be ready by now so add those too. For a golden-brown colour, I grilled my halloumi and broccoli for about 6 minutes, making sure to flip the cheese over to cook it evenly.

Don't forget to check on the quinoa. It should be ready once the water is gone (about 7-8 minutes), but taste to be sure (it should have a somewhat crunchy texture). Once the halloumi, broccoli, and quinoa are ready, throw everything into your salad bowl and mix well. Season with some olive oil and serve while the halloumi is hot.

Black Bean Lentil Salad With Lime Dressing

Preparation time: 5 mins.
Cooking time: 0 mins.
Ingredient:
1 cup green/brown lentils (uncooked)
15 oz. can black beans
1 red bell pepper
1/2 small red onion
1-2 roma tomatoes
2/3 cup cilantro (stems removed)
Optional: green onion.
Juice of 1 lime
2 Tbsp. olive oil (omit for oil-free)
1 tsp. Dijon mustard
1-2 cloves garlic (minced)
1 tsp. cumin
1/2 tsp. oregano
1/8 tsp. salt
Optional: chipotle powder, chili powder, pepper, hot sauce, other seasonings, etc.
Directions:

Cook lentils according to package directions, leaving firm not mushy. Drain.

While lentils are cooking, make the dressing: place all ingredients in a small bowl and whisk to combine. Set aside. Finely dice the bell pepper, onion, and tomatoes. Roughly chop the cilantro. In a large bowl, place the black beans (rinsed and drained), bell pepper, onion, tomatoes, and lentils. Add the dressing and toss to combine. Add cilantro, and lightly toss. Serve immediately or chill covered in the fridge for at least an hour to let the flavors combine.

Arugula Lentil Salad

Preparation time: 5 mins.
Cooking time: 5 mins.
Ingredient:
¾ cups cashews
1 onion
3 tbsp olive oil
1 chilli / jalapeño
5-6 sun-dried tomatoes in oil
3 slices bread (whole wheat)
1 cup brown lentils, cooked
1 handful arugula/rocket
2 tbsp balsamic vinegar
salt and pepper to taste.
Directions:
Roast the cashews on a low heat for about three minutes in a pan to maximize aroma. Then throw them into the salad bowl. Dice up and fry the onion in one third of the olive oil for about 3 minutes on a low heat. Meanwhile chop the chilli/jalapeño and dried tomatoes. Add them to the pan and fry for another 1-2 minutes. Cut the bread into big croutons. Move the onion mix into a big bowl. Now add the rest of the oil to the pan and fry the chopped-up bread until crunchy. Season with salt and pepper. Wash the arugula and add it to the bowl. Put the lentils in too, and mix them all around. Season with salt, pepper and balsamic vinegar. Serve with the croutons. Super tasty!

Red Cabbage Salad With Curried Seitan

Preparation time: 10 mins
Cooking time: 10 mins
Ingredient:
1 Tbs. olive oil
1 8-oz. pkg. seitan, cut into bite-size strips
3 cloves garlic, minced
¾ tsp. mild curry powder
6 cups shredded red cabbage
1 small cucumber, sliced into thin half-moons
3 green onions, thinly sliced
⅓ cup prepared mango chutney
⅓ cup creamy natural peanut butter.
Directions:
To make Dressing: Blend chutney, peanut butter, and 1/3 cup water in blender until smooth. Set aside. To make Salad: Heat 2 tsp. oil in large skillet over medium heat. Add seitan, and season with salt, if desired. Sauté 5 to 7 minutes, or until browned. Add garlic and remaining 1 tsp. oil, and sauté 30 seconds. Sprinkle with curry powder, and sauté 2 minutes more. Remove from heat, and keep warm. Toss cabbage and cucumber with Dressing in large bowl. Top with warm seitan and green onions.

Chickpea, Red Kidney Bean And Feta Salad

Preparation time: 5 mins
Cooking time: 5 mins
Ingredient:
1 can chickpeas
1 can red kidney beans
1 piece small of ginger grated or shredded
1 medium onion diced
2- 3 cloves garlic
1 tbsp olive oil
A pinch of red chili flakes
3-4 spring onions green part only, chopped, scallions
1 cup chopped parsley OR coriander I used cilantro
Juice of one lemon
150 g feta cheese – almost half cup size
Salt and Black pepper.
Directions:
Heat 1 tablespoon of olive oil and cook the onion till lightly golden. Do not overdo it and the onions should still be crunchy. Add garlic, ginger and chili and cook till the garlic is fragrant. Set aside to cool so it doesn't melt the feta when you mix it in. Drain the chickpeas and red kidney beans, rinse and place in the salad bowl. Add crumbled feta, spring onion, parsley (or

coriander) and lemon juice, season with salt and pepper. Add the cooled onion and garlic mixture and remaining oil and mix well.

Curried Carrot Slaw With Tempeh

Preparation time: 10 mins
Cooking time: 10 mins
Ingredient:
8 ounces tempeh, sliced into triangles
1/4 tsp liquid smoke (optional)
1 1/2 Tbsp maple syrup, grade B
1 tsp extra virgin olive oil or virgin coconut oil
2-3 tsp tamari or 2 tsp soy sauce
1 Tbsp crushed raw walnuts
4 cups shredded carrots
1 small onion, diced
1 Tbsp curry powder
1/4 tsp turmeric powder (for added turmeric power, optional)
1/8 tsp black pepper
2 Tbsp tahini
1/4 cup fresh lemon juice
sweet stuff: 1 – 1 1/2 Tbsp maple syrup + an optional handful or raisins
1/2 cup flat leaf parsley, finely chopped + some for garnish
a few pinches of cayenne for heat (optional)
salt and pepper for carrot salad – to taste.
Directions:
Warm a skillet up over high heat and add in the coconut or olive oil. When oil is hot, add the tempeh triangles, tamari, maple and liquid smoke. Flip the tempeh around a bit to allow it to absorb the liquid. Cook for about 5 minutes, flipping the tempeh a few times throughout the cooking process. When tempeh is browned and edges blackened a bit, and all liquid absorbed, turn off heat. Sprinkle the walnut pieces and some black pepper over top the tempeh and set pan aside to keep triangles warm in skillet. In a large mixing bowl, add the carrots, tahini, lemon juice, spices, parsley, maple syrup, optional raisins and onion. Toss very well for a few minutes to marinate the carrots with the dressing. For a creamier salad, add another spoonful of tahini. To thin things out and make the salad zestier, add another splash of lemon juice or a teaspoon of apple cider vinegar. Finally, add salt and pepper to the carrot salad to taste. Pour the carrot salad in a large serving bowl and top with the tempeh. Serve right away or place in the fridge to serve in a few hours or up to a day later. The carrots will soften the longer they set in the fridge.

Black & White Bean Quinoa Salad

Preparation time: 15 mins
Cooking time: 15 mins
Ingredient:
⅓ cup (75 mL) quinoa
1 can (19 oz/540 mL) black beans, drained and rinsed
1 can (19 oz/540 mL) navy beans, drained and rinsed
1 cup (250 mL) diced cucumbers
¼ cup (50 mL) diced red onion
1 jalapeno pepper, seeded and minced (I've never used it and find the dish spicy enough for me, but feel free to add it if you like things hot!)
¼ cup (50 mL) chopped fresh coriander (cilantro)
¼ cup (50 mL) vegetable oil (I use cold pressed extra-virgin olive oil)
2 tbsp (25 mL) lime juice
1 tbsp (15 mL) cider vinegar
1 clove garlic, minced
½ tsp (2 mL) chili powder
1 tsp (5 mL) ground coriander
½ tsp (2 mL) dried oregano
¼ tsp (1 mL) salt
¼ tsp (1 mL) pepper.
Directions:
In saucepan of boiling salted ⅔ C water, cook quinoa until tender, about 12 minutes. Drain and rinse. Dressing: In large bowl, whisk together oil, lime juice, vinegar, garlic, chili powder, coriander, oregano, salt and pepper. Add quinoa, black beans, navy beans, cucumber, onion, jalapeño pepper and coriander; toss to combine.

Greek Salad With Seitan Gyros Strips

Preparation time: 5 mins
Cooking time: 5 mins
Ingredient: 4 tomatoes
1 punnet cherry tomatoes
1 1/2 crunchy cucumbers

49

1 big handful kalamata olives
1/2 Spanish onion finely sliced
1/4 stick of Cheesy mozzarella style cheese.
Fresh oregano and mint
1/4 cup good quality extra virgin olive oil
2 Tablespoons vinegar (red wine or balsamic)
1 teaspoon castor sugar
2 teaspoons mixed dried Italian herbs
1 clove finely chopped garlic
1 teaspoon soy sauce
Salt, pepper.
Directions:

In a small frying pan, place gyros strips and fry until slightly blackened on the edges. Leave to cool. Cut up all your veggies roughly and place in a large bowl. Add olives, oregano, mint and chopped cheese. In a jar add all dressing ingredients. Shake well and taste. Combine the cooled gyros strips, salad and dressing and coat well.

Chickpea And Edamame Salad

Preparation time: 30 mins
Cooking time: 30 mins
Ingredient: 2 15.5oz each cans chickpea (garbanzo beans) rinsed and drained
3/4 cup edamame soy beans
1/3 cup chopped red pepper
1/3 cup chopped green pepper
1/4 cup diced carrots
3 tablespoons dried cranberries
1 garlic clove minced
Dressing
2 tablespoons grapeseed oil
2 tablespoons olive oil
1 teaspoon white distilled vinegar
1 teaspoon sugar
1/4 teaspoon dried oregano
1/4 teaspoon dried basil
1/4 teaspoon dried rosemary
Salt and pepper
Directions:

In a large bowl combine chickpeas, edamame, red pepper, green pepper, carrots, dried cranberries, minced garlic and set aside. In a small bowl combine grapeseed oil, olive oil, vinegar, sugar, oregano, basil and rosemary. Whisk until blended. Pour dressing over chick peas and gently toss. Season with salt and pepper to taste. Chill for at least 30 minutes for flavors to blend. Serve chilled.

Lunch Recipes

Teriyaki Tofu Stir-Fry

Preparation time: 10 minutes
Cooking Time: 20 minutes
Serving: 4
Ingredients:
For the Tofu:
2 tablespoons chopped green onions
2 cups asparagus
14 ounces (397 grams) tofu, firm, pressed
2 teaspoons red chili sauce
1 tablespoon soy sauce
3 teaspoons olive oil
For the Sauce:
2 tablespoons minced garlic
1 ½ tablespoons rice vinegar
1/2 tablespoon grated ginger
2 teaspoons corn starch
1/4 cup (59 grams) coconut sugar
3 tablespoons soy sauce
1 tablespoon sesame oil
1/2 cup (118 ml) water
For Serving:
4 cups (946 grams) quinoa, cooked
Directions:
Prepare the tofu: pat dry tofu and cut into ½-inch cubes.

Take a medium skillet pan, place it over medium-high heat, add 1 teaspoon oil and when hot, add tofu cubes in a single layer, then cook for 3 to 4 minutes until golden brown.

Transfer tofu pieces to a large bowl, add 1 teaspoon oil in the pan and repeat with the remaining tofu cubes.

Meanwhile, prepare the sauce: take a small bowl, add all of the sauce ingredients in it and whisk until combined, then set aside until required.

When all the tofu gets cooked, drizzle them with sauces and toss until coated, set aside until required.

Wipe clean the skillet pan, return it over medium-high heat, add remaining oil and when hot, add asparagus and green onions, then cook for 3 minutes until tender-crisp.

Return tofu pieces into the pan, drizzle with prepared sauce, switch heat to medium level, toss until all the ingredients are mixed, and cook for 3 to 5 minutes until the sauce starts to thicken.

When done, taste to adjust the seasoning of the sauce and then remove the pan from heat.

Distribute cooked quinoa among plates, top with tofu and vegetables, and then serve.

Nutrition: 411 Cal; 11 g Fat; 1 g Saturated Fat; 58 g Carbs; 8 g Fiber; 19 g Protein; 12 g Sugar

Red Lentil And Quinoa Fritters

Preparation Time: 20 minutes
Cooking Time: 25 minutes
Serving: 10
Ingredients:
For the Fritters:
1/4 cup (59 grams) chickpea flour
1 ½ cups (354 grams) quinoa
1/4 cup (59 grams) cornmeal
1/2 cup (118 grams) red lentils
2 teaspoons ground turmeric
1/8 teaspoon black bell pepper
1/2 teaspoon salt
1/4 cup (59 grams) chopped parsley
1 teaspoon cumin
1/4 teaspoon ground cinnamon
1/2 of a lemon, juiced

1 tablespoon Dijon mustard
1/4 cup (59 grams) tahini
4 cups (946 ml) vegetable broth
For the Sauce:
1 teaspoon minced garlic
1/4 teaspoon salt
1 tablespoon chopped dill
3 tablespoons tahini
1 lemon, juiced
1 cup coconut yogurt, unsweetened
Directions:

Switch on the oven, set it to 400° F and let it preheat.

Take a medium pot, place it over medium-high heat, add lentils and quinoa, pour in vegetable broth, and bring it to a boil.

Switch heat to medium-low level and simmer the grains for 15 minutes until cooked, covering the pot.

When done, let grains cool for 10 minutes, fluff them with a fork and transfer into a large bowl.

Add remaining ingredients for the fritters in it and stir well until incorporated.

Shape the mixture into ten patties, arrange them on a baking sheet lined with aluminum foil and bake for 25 minutes until golden brown on both sides and thoroughly cooked, turning halfway.

Meanwhile, prepare the yogurt sauce: take a medium bowl, place all the ingredients for it inside and whisk until combined.

Serve fritters with yogurt sauce.

Nutrition: 173 Cal; 4 g Fat; 1 g Saturated Fat; 27 g Carbs; 2 g Fiber; 7 g Protein; 3 g Sugar

Green Pea Fritters

Preparation Time: 10 minutes
Cooking Time: 25 minutes
Serving: 4
Ingredients:
For the Fritters:
1 ½ cups (140 grams) chickpea flour
2 cups (250 grams) frozen peas
1 large white onion, peeled, diced
1 tablespoon minced garlic
1/8 teaspoon salt
1 teaspoon baking soda
2 tablespoons mixed dried Italian herbs
1 tablespoon olive oil
Water as needed
For the Yoghurt Sauce:
1/2 teaspoon dried rosemary
1/2 teaspoon dried parsley
1/2 teaspoon dried mint
1 lemon, juiced
1 cup soy yogurt

Directions:

Switch on the oven, set it to 350° F and let it preheat.

Take a medium saucepan, place it over medium heat, add peas, cover them with water, bring it to a boil, cook for 2 to 3 minutes until tender, and when done, drain the peas and set aside until required.

Take a frying pan, place it over medium heat, add oil and when hot, add onion and garlic; cook for 5 minutes until softened.

Transfer onion-garlic mixture to a food processor, add peas and pulse for 1 minute until the thick paste comes together.

Tip the mixture in a bowl, add salt, baking soda, Italian herbs, and chickpea flour, stir until incorporated and shape the mixture into ten patties.

Brush the patties with oil, arrange them onto a baking sheet and bake for 15 to 18 minutes until golden brown and thoroughly cooked, turning halfway.

Meanwhile, prepare the yogurt sauce: take a medium bowl, add all the ingredients for it and whisk until combined.

Serve fritters with prepared yogurt sauce.

Nutrition: 94 Cal; 2 g Fat; 0 g Saturated Fat; 14 g Carbs; 3 g Fiber; 4 g Protein; 2 g Sugar

Breaded Tofu Steaks

Preparation Time: 10 minutes
Cooking Time: 12 minutes
Serving: 4
Ingredients:
3 cups (750 grams) tofu, extra-firm, pressed
4 tablespoons tomato paste
2 ½ tablespoons minced garlic
1 cup (236 grams) panko breadcrumbs and more as needed
½ teaspoon ground black pepper
2 tablespoon maple syrup
2 tablespoon Dijon mustard
2 tablespoon soy sauce
4 tablespoons olive oil
2 tablespoon water
BBQ sauce for serving
Directions:
Prepare the tofu steaks: pat dry tofu and then cut them into four slices.

Prepare the sauce: take a medium bowl, add garlic, black pepper, maple syrup, mustard, tomato paste, soy sauce, and water; stir until combined.

Take a shallow dish and place bread crumbs on it.

Working on one tofu steak at a time, first coat it with prepared sauce, then dredge it with bread crumbs until evenly coated and place it on a plate.

Repeat with the remaining tofu slices.

Take a frying pan, place it over medium heat, pour oil in it and when hot, place a tofu steak inside and cook for 4 to 6 minutes per side until golden brown and cooked.

Transfer tofu steak to a plate and repeat with the remaining tofu steaks.

Serve tofu steaks with the BBQ sauce.

Nutrition: 419.4 Cal; 23.9 g Fat; 3.9 g Saturated Fat; 33.3 g Carbs; 4.3 g Fiber; 22.8 g Protein; 3 g Sugar;

Thai Tofu And Quinoa Bowls

Preparation Time: 15 minutes
Cooking Time: 20 minutes
Serving: 4
Ingredients:
3/4 cup (177 grams) quinoa, cooked
1 cup (236 grams) frozen edamame, thawed
12 ounces (175 grams) tofu, extra-firm, pressed
2 medium carrots, grated
1 green onion, sliced
1/2 teaspoon minced garlic
2 teaspoons grated ginger
1/2 cup chopped cilantro
1/2 teaspoon red chili flakes
1 tablespoon soy sauce
2 teaspoons agave syrup
2 tablespoons lime juice
2 tablespoons peanut butter
1 tablespoon water
4 teaspoons sesame seeds, toasted
Directions:
Switch on the oven, set it to 400° F and let it preheat.

Prepare the tofu: cut tofu into ¾-inch cubes.

Take a large baking sheet, line it with foil, spread tofu pieces on it, and bake for 20 minutes until golden brown, stirring halfway.

Prepare the drizzle: take a small bowl, place garlic, ginger, chili flakes, soy sauce, agave syrup, butter, lime, and water in it and then whisk until combined.

After tofu gets cooked, let it cool for 10 minutes and transfer into a large bowl.

Add carrot, green onions, cilantro, cabbage, and edamame, drizzle with the prepared dressing and sprinkle with sesame seeds.

Mix quinoa with salad and serve.

Nutrition: 330 Cal; 13 g Fat; 3 g Saturated Fat; 36 g Carbs; 7 g Fiber; 19 g Protein; 10 g Sugar;

Cauliflower Steaks

Preparation Time: 10 minutes
Cooking Time: 30 minutes
Serving: 3
Ingredients:
2 medium heads of cauliflower
1 teaspoon garlic powder

1/2 teaspoon ground black pepper
1 teaspoon salt
1 teaspoon coriander
1 teaspoon paprika
2 tablespoons olive oil
For Serving:
1 cup (236 grams) hummus
Directions:
Switch on the oven, set it to 425° F and let it preheat.

Cut each cauliflower head into three slices, brush them with oil on both sides and sprinkle with garlic powder, black pepper, salt, coriander, and paprika.

Take a large baking sheet, line it with aluminum foil, arrange cauliflower steaks on it and then bake for 30 minutes until tender and golden brown on both sides.

Serve straight away.

Nutrition: 149 Cal; 9 g Fat; 1 g Saturated Fat; 14 g Carbs; 7 g Fiber; 5 g Protein; 3 g Sugar;

Avocado And Hummus Sandwich

Preparation Time: 5 minutes
Cooking Time: 0 minutes
Serving: 1
Ingredients:
2 slices of whole-wheat bread sliced
4 slices of tomato
1 lettuce leaf
1/2 avocado, sliced
2 tablespoons cilantro leaves
2 teaspoons hot sauce
3 tablespoon hummus

Directions:
Take a slice of bread, spread hummus on its one side, then top with avocado slices and drizzle with hot sauce.

Scatter tomato slice on top of avocado slices, then top with lettuce and cilantro and cover with the other slice of bread.

Serve straight away.

Nutrition: 302 Cal; 5.7 g Fat; 1.1 g Saturated Fat; 49.8 g Carbs; 12 g Fiber; 12.8 g Protein; 7.8 g Sugar

Chickpea Spinach Salad

Preparation Time: 10 minutes
Cooking Time: 0 minutes
Serving: 2
Ingredients:
12 ounces (340 grams) cooked chickpeas
1/4 cup (59 grams) raisins
1 cup (236 grams) spinach
1/2 teaspoon red chili flakes
1/8 teaspoon salt
1 teaspoon cumin
3 teaspoons agave syrup
1/2 tablespoon lemon juice
4 tablespoons olive oil
3 ½ ounces (99 grams) vegan parmesan cheese

Directions:
Take a large salad bowl, add chickpeas and spinach in it, then add cheese and toss until mixed.

Prepare the dressing: take a small bowl, add raisins in it along with salt, pepper, cumin, lemon juice, agave syrup and oil and whisk until combined.

Drizzle the dressing over salad, toss until well coated, and serve.

Nutrition: 658 Cal; 40 g Fat; 11 g Saturated Fat; 52 g Carbs; 9.7 g Fiber; 23 g Protein; 15.2 g Sugar

Quinoa Buddha Bowl

Preparation Time: 10 Minutes
Cooking Time: 0 minutes
Servings: 1
Ingredients:
Avocado (1, Diced)
Cooked Quinoa (.75 C.)
Pico de Gallo (3 T.)
Hummus (.25 C.)
Black Beans (.75 C.)
Lime Juice (1 T.)
Directions:
Before you begin this recipe, you will want to cook your quinoa ahead of time according to the directions on the package.

Once the quinoa is cooked, mix it in a bowl with the beans and the hummus. Stir everything together before squeezing in the lime juice.

Finally, top the bowl off with avocado and Pico de Gallo, and lunch is served.

Nutrition: Calories: 26 Proteins: 26gCarbs: 30g Fats: 20g

Simple Curried Vegetable Rice

Preparation Time: 30 Minutes
Cooking Time: 10 Minutes
Servings: 4
Ingredients:
Carrots (2, Chopped)
Spinach (1 C., Chopped)
Ginger (2 t.)
Broccoli (1, Chopped)
Salt (to Taste)
Cooked Brown Rice (1 C.)
Garlic (2, Minced)
Pepper (to Taste)
Curry Powder (1 t.)

Directions:
Before you begin cooking, you will want to take some prep time to chop up all of your vegetables beforehand. When they are cut into smaller pieces, this means they will cook faster!

Once your ingredients are prepared, take out a pan and begin to heat it over a medium heat. Once warm, add in some olive oil and then sprinkle in the garlic and the ginger.

Next, you will want to add in the broccoli and carrots. At this point, season with salt and pepper and cook for two minutes.

Once the vegetables are cooked to your liking, add in the cooked brown rice along with the curry powder and toss the ingredients until everything is well coated.

Finally, add in the spinach and cook for another minute or until it becomes wilted. Season with some more salt and pepper, and then your meal will be ready just like that!

Nutrition: Calories: 280 Proteins: 10g Carbs: 50g Fats: 5g

Spicy Southwestern Hummus Wraps

Preparation Time: 15 Minutes
Cooking Time: 0 Minutes
Servings: 1
Ingredients:
Whole-wheat Wrap (1)
Lettuce (1 C., Shredded)
Tomato (1 T., Diced)
Hummus (4 T.)
Avocado (2 T., Diced)
Corn (2 T.)
Black Beans (2 T.)
Directions:

For a quick lunch, simply lay out your wrap and spread the hummus over the surface.

Once the hummus is in place, layer the rest of the ingredients and then roll the wrap up before eating.

Nutrition: Calories: 400 Proteins: 15g Carbs: 50g Fats: 15g

Buffalo Cauliflower Wings

Preparation Time: 30 Minutes
Cooking Time: 15 Minutes
Servings: 4
Ingredients:
Chickpea Flour (.75 C)
Almond Milk (1 C.)
Buffalo Sauce (1 C.)
Cauliflower (1 Head)
Curry Powder (1 t.)
Onion Powder (1 t.)
Garlic Powder (1 t.)
Nutritional Yeast (2 T.)

Directions:
You will want to begin this recipe by prepping the oven to 450. As this warms up, go ahead and prep a baking sheet with parchment paper and then set it to the side.

Next, you are going to take a bowl and combine the nutritional yeast and spices with the flour.

With your flour made up, carefully dip the cauliflower into the soymilk and directly into the flour. Once the cauliflower piece is well coated, place it onto your baking sheet and continue until you have covered every cauliflower floret.

When you are ready, pop the baking dish into the oven for about twenty minutes. After this time, the cauliflower should be crispy.

Once the cauliflower is cooked through, place it into a bowl, and toss with the hot sauce. When all of the pieces are well coated, place them back into the oven for another ten minutes, and then they will be ready.

Nutrition: Calories: 160 Proteins: 11g Carbs: 20g Fats: 3g

Avocado, Spinach and Kale Soup

Preparation time: 10 minutes
Cooking time: 0 minutes
Servings: 4
Ingredients:
2 avocados, pitted, peeled and cut in halves
4 cups vegetable stock
2 tablespoons cilantro, chopped
Juice of 1 lime
1 teaspoon rosemary, dried
½ cup spinach leaves
½ cup kale, torn
Salt and black pepper to the taste
Directions:
In a blender, combine the avocados with the stock and the other ingredients, pulse well, divide into bowls and serve for lunch.

Nutrition: calories 300, fat 23, fiber 5, carbs 6, protein 7

Curry spinach soup

Preparation time: 10 minutes
Cooking time: 0 minutes
Servings: 4
Ingredients:
1 cup almond milk
1 tablespoon green curry paste
1 pound spinach leaves
1 tablespoon cilantro, chopped
Salt and black pepper to the taste
4 cups veggie stock
1 tablespoon cilantro, chopped
Directions:
In your blender, combine the almond milk with the curry paste and the other ingredients, pulse well, divide into bowls and serve for lunch.
Nutrition: calories 240, fat 4, fiber 2, carbs 6, protein 2

Arugula and Artichokes Bowls

Preparation time: 5 minutes
Cooking time: 0 minutes
Servings: 4
Ingredients:
2 cups baby arugula
¼ cup walnuts, chopped
1 cup canned artichoke hearts, drained and quartered
1 tablespoon balsamic vinegar
2 tablespoons cilantro, chopped
2 tablespoons olive oil
Salt and black pepper to the taste
1 tablespoon lemon juice

Directions:
In a bowl, combine the artichokes with the arugula, walnuts and the other ingredients, toss, divide into smaller bowls and serve for lunch.
Nutrition: calories 200, fat 2, fiber 1, carbs 5, protein 7

Spinach and Broccoli Soup

Preparation time: 10 minutes
Cooking time: 20 minutes
Servings: 4
Ingredients:
3 shallots, chopped
1 tablespoon olive oil
2 garlic cloves, minced
½ pound broccoli florets
½ pound baby spinach
Salt and black pepper to the taste
4 cups veggie stock
1 teaspoon turmeric powder
1 tablespoon lime juice
Directions:
Heat up a pot with the oil over medium high heat, add the shallots and the garlic and sauté for 5 minutes.
Add the broccoli, spinach and the other ingredients, toss, bring to a simmer and cook over medium heat for 15 minutes.
Ladle into soup bowls and serve.
Nutrition: calories 150, fat 3, fiber 1, carbs 3, protein 7

Coconut zucchini cream

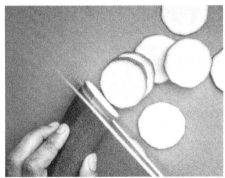

Preparation time: 10 minutes
Cooking time: 25 minutes
Servings: 4
Ingredients:
1 pound zucchinis, roughly chopped
2 tablespoons avocado oil
4 scallions, chopped
Salt and black pepper to the taste
6 cups veggie stock

57

1 teaspoon basil, dried
1 teaspoon cumin, ground
3 garlic cloves, minced
¾ cup coconut cream
1 tablespoon dill, chopped
Directions:

Heat up a pot with the oil over medium high heat, add the scallions and the garlic and sauté for 5 minutes.

Add the rest of the ingredients, stir, bring to a simmer and cook over medium heat for 20 minutes more.

Blend the soup using an immersion blender, ladle into bowls and serve.

Nutrition: calories 160, fat 4, fiber 2, carbs 4, protein n 8

Zucchini and Cauliflower Soup

Preparation time: 10 minutes
Cooking time: 25 minutes
Servings: 4
Ingredients:
4 scallions, chopped
1 teaspoon ginger, grated
2 tablespoons olive oil
1 pound zucchinis, sliced
2 cups cauliflower florets
Salt and black pepper to the taste
6 cups veggie stock
1 garlic clove, minced
1 tablespoon lemon juice
1 cup coconut cream
Directions:

Heat up a pot with the oil over medium heat, add the scallions, ginger and the garlic and sauté for 5 minutes.

Add the rest of the ingredients, bring to a simmer and cook over medium heat for 20 minutes.

Blend everything using an immersion blender, ladle into soup bowls and serve.

Nutrition: calories 154, fat 12, fiber 3, carbs 5, protein 4

Chard soup

Preparation time: 10 minutes
Cooking time: 25 minutes
Servings: 4
Ingredients:
1 pound Swiss chard, chopped
½ cup shallots, chopped
1 tablespoon avocado oil
1 teaspoon cumin, ground
1 teaspoon rosemary, dried
1 teaspoon basil, dried
2 garlic cloves, minced
Salt and black pepper to the taste
6 cups vegetable stock
1 tablespoon tomato passata
1 tablespoon cilantro, chopped
Directions:

Heat up a pan with the oil over medium heat, add the shallots and the garlic and sauté for 5 minutes.

Add the swiss chard and the other ingredients, toss, bring to a simmer and cook over medium heat for 20 minutes more.

Divide the soup into bowls and serve.

Nutrition: calories 232, fat 23, fiber 3, carbs 4, protein 3

Avocado, Pine Nuts and Chard Salad

Preparation time: 5 minutes
Cooking time: 15 minutes
Servings: 4
Ingredients:
1 pound swiss chard, roughly chopped
2 tablespoons olive oil
1 avocado, peeled, pitted and roughly cubed
2 spring onions, chopped
¼ Cup pine nuts, toasted
1 tablespoon balsamic vinegar

Salt and black pepper to the taste
Directions:

Heat up a pan with the oil over medium heat, add the spring onions, pine nuts and the chard, stir and sauté for 5 minutes.

Add the vinegar and the other ingredients, toss, cook over medium heat for 10 minutes more, divide into bowls and serve for lunch.

Nutrition: calories 120, fat 2, fiber 1, carbs 4, protein 8

Grapes, Avocado and Spinach Salad

Preparation time: 10 minutes
Cooking time: 0 minutes
Servings: 4
Ingredients:
1 cup green grapes, halved
2 cups baby spinach
1 avocado, pitted, peeled and cubed
Salt and black pepper to the taste
2 tablespoons olive oil
1 tablespoon thyme, chopped
1 tablespoon rosemary, chopped
1 tablespoon lime juice
1 garlic clove, minced
Directions:

In a salad bowl, combine the grapes with the spinach and the other ingredients, toss, and serve for lunch.

Nutrition: calories 190, fat 17.1, fiber 4.6, carbs 10.9, protein 1.7

Greens and Olives Pan

Preparation time: 10 minutes
Cooking time: 15 minutes
Servings: 4
Ingredients:
4 spring onions, chopped
2 tablespoons olive oil
½ cup green olives, pitted and halved
¼ cup pine nuts, toasted
1 tablespoon balsamic vinegar
2 cups baby spinach
1 cup baby arugula
1 cup asparagus, trimmed, blanched and halved
Salt and black pepper to the taste
Directions:

Heat up a pan with the oil over medium high heat, add the spring onions and the asparagus and sauté for 5 minutes.

Add the olives, spinach and the other ingredients, toss, cook over medium heat for 10 minutes, divide between plates and serve for lunch.

Nutrition: calories 136, fat 13.1, fiber 1.9, carbs 4.4, protein 2.8

Mushrooms and Chard Soup

Preparation time: 10 minutes
Cooking time: 30 minutes
Servings: 4
Ingredients:
3 cups Swiss chard, chopped
6 cups vegetable stock
1 cup mushrooms, sliced
2 garlic cloves, minced
1 tablespoon olive oil
2 scallions, chopped
2 tablespoons balsamic vinegar
¼ cup basil, chopped
Salt and black pepper to the taste
1 tablespoon cilantro, chopped
Directions:

Heat up a pot with the oil over medium high heat, add the scallions and the garlic and sauté for 5 minutes.

Add the mushrooms and sauté for another 5 minutes.

Add the rest of the ingredients, toss, bring to a simmer and cook over medium heat for 20 minutes more.

Ladle the soup into bowls and serve.

Nutrition: calories 140, fat 4, fiber 2, carbs 4, protein 8

Tomato, Green Beans and Chard Soup

Preparation time: 10 minutes
Cooking time: 35 minutes
Servings: 4
Ingredients:
2 scallions, chopped
1 cup swiss chard, chopped
1 tablespoon olive oil
1 red bell pepper, chopped
Salt and black pepper to the taste
1 cup tomatoes, cubed
1 cup green beans, chopped
6 cups vegetable stock
2 tablespoons tomato passata
2 garlic cloves, minced
2 teaspoons thyme, chopped
½ Teaspoon red pepper flakes
Directions:
Heat up a pot with the oil over medium heat, add the scallions, garlic and the pepper flakes and sauté for 5 minutes.

Add the chard and the other ingredients, toss, bring to a simmer and cook over medium heat for 30 minutes more.

Ladle the soup into bowls and serve for lunch.

Nutrition: calories 150, fat 8, fiber 2, carbs 4, protein 9

Hot roasted peppers cream

Preparation time: 10 minutes
Cooking time: 30 minutes
Servings: 4
Ingredients:
1 red chili pepper, minced
4 garlic cloves, minced
2 pounds mixed bell peppers, roasted, peeled and chopped
4 scallions, chopped
1 cup coconut cream

Salt and black pepper to the taste
2 tablespoons olive oil
½ tablespoon basil, chopped
4 cups vegetable stock
¼ cup chives, chopped
Directions:
Heat up a pot with the oil over medium heat, add the garlic and the chili pepper and sauté for 5 minutes.

Add the peppers and the other ingredients, toss, bring to a simmer and cook over medium heat for 25 minutes.

Blend the soup using an immersion blender, divide into bowls and serve.

Nutrition: calories 140, fat 2, fiber 2, carbs 5, protein 8

Eggplant and Peppers Soup

Preparation time: 10 minutes
Cooking time: 40 minutes
Servings: 4
Ingredients:
2 red bell peppers, chopped
3 scallions, chopped
3 garlic cloves, minced
2 tablespoon olive oil
Salt and black pepper to the taste
5 cups vegetable stock
1 bay leaf
½ cup coconut cream
1 pound eggplants, roughly cubed
2 tablespoons basil, chopped
Directions:
Heat up a pot with the oil over medium heat, add the scallions and the garlic and sauté for 5 minutes.

Add the peppers and the eggplants and sauté for 5 minutes more.

Add the remaining ingredients, toss, bring to a simmer, cook for 30 minutes, ladle into bowls and serve for lunch.

Nutrition: calories 180, fat 2, fiber 3, carbs 5, protein 10

Eggplant and Olives Stew

Preparation time: 10 minutes
Cooking time: 30 minutes
Servings: 4
Ingredients:
2 scallions, chopped
2 tablespoons avocado oil
2 garlic cloves, chopped
1 bunch parsley, chopped
Salt and black pepper to the taste
1 teaspoon basil, dried
1 teaspoon cumin, dried
2 eggplants, roughly cubed
1 cup green olives, pitted and sliced
3 tablespoons balsamic vinegar
½ Cup tomato passata

Directions:
Heat up a pot with the oil over medium heat, add the scallions, garlic, basil and cumin and sauté for 5 minutes.
Add the eggplants and the other ingredients, toss, cook over medium heat for 25 minutes more, divide into bowls and serve.
Nutrition: calories 93, fat 1.8, fiber 10.6, carbs 18.6, protein 3.4

Cauliflower and Artichokes Soup

Preparation time: 10 minutes
Cooking time: 25 minutes
Servings: 4
Ingredients:
1 pound cauliflower florets
1 cup canned artichoke hearts, drained and chopped
2 scallions, chopped
2 tablespoons olive oil
2 garlic cloves, minced
6 cups vegetable stock
Salt and black pepper to the taste
2/3 cup coconut cream
2 tablespoons cilantro, chopped
Directions:
Heat up a pot with the oil over medium heat, add the scallions and the garlic and sauté for 5 minutes.
Add the cauliflower and the other ingredients, toss, bring to a simmer and cook over medium heat for 20 minutes more.
Blend the soup using an immersion blender, divide it into bowls and serve.
Nutrition: calories 207, fat 17.2, fiber 6.2, carbs 14.1, protein 4.7

Cauliflower Latke

Preparation Time: 15 minutes
Cooking Time: 30 minutes
Servings: 4
Ingredients:
12 oz. cauliflower rice, cooked
1 egg, beaten
1/3 cup cornstarch
Salt and pepper to taste
¼ cup vegetable oil, divided
Chopped onion chives
Direction
Squeeze excess water from the cauliflower rice using paper towels.
Place the cauliflower rice in a bowl.
Stir in the egg and cornstarch.
Season with salt and pepper.
Pour 2 tablespoons of oil into a pan over medium heat.
Add 2 to 3 tablespoons of the cauliflower mixture into the pan.
Cook for 3 minutes per side or until golden.
Repeat until you've used up the rest of the batter.
Garnish with chopped chives.
Nutrition: Calories: 209 Total fat: 15.2g Saturated fat: 1.4g Cholesterol: 47mg Sodium: 331mg Potassium: 21mg Carbohydrates: 13.4g Fiber: 1.9g Sugar: 2g Protein: 3.4g

Roasted Brussels Sprouts

Preparation Time: 30 minutes
Cooking Time: 20 minutes
Servings: 4
Ingredients:
1 lb. Brussels sprouts, sliced in half
1 shallot, chopped
1 tablespoon olive oil
Salt and pepper to taste
2 teaspoons balsamic vinegar
¼ cup pomegranate seeds
¼ cup goat cheese, crumbled
Direction:
Preheat your oven to 400 degrees F.
Coat the Brussels sprouts with oil.
Sprinkle with salt and pepper.
Transfer to a baking pan.
Roast in the oven for 20 minutes.
Drizzle with the vinegar.
Sprinkle with the seeds and cheese before serving.
Nutrition: Calories: 117 Total fat: 5.7g Saturated fat: 1.8g Cholesterol: 4mg Sodium: 216mg Potassium: 491mg Carbohydrates: 13.6g Fiber: 4.8g Sugar: 5g Protein: 5.8g

Brussels Sprouts & Cranberries Salad

Preparation Time: 10 minutes
Cooking Time: 0 minute
Servings: 6
Ingredients:
3 tablespoons lemon juice
¼ cup olive oil
Salt and pepper to taste
1 lb. Brussels sprouts, sliced thinly
¼ cup dried cranberries, chopped
½ cup pecans, toasted and chopped
½ cup vegan parmesan cheese, shaved
Direction
Mix the lemon juice, olive oil, salt and pepper in a bowl.

Toss the Brussels sprouts, cranberries and pecans in this mixture.
Sprinkle the Parmesan cheese on top.
Nutrition: Calories 245 Total Fat 18.9 g Saturated Fat 9 g Cholesterol 3 mg Sodium 350 mg Total Carbohydrate 15.9 g Dietary Fiber 5 g Protein 6.4 g Total Sugars 10 g Potassium 20 mg

Potato Latke

Preparation Time: 15 minutes
Cooking Time: 10 minutes
Servings: 6
Ingredients:
1 onion, grated
1 ½ teaspoons baking powder
Salt and pepper to taste
2 lb. potatoes, peeled and grated
¼ cup all-purpose flour
4 tablespoons vegetable oil
Chopped onion chives
Direction
Preheat your oven to 400 degrees F.
In a bowl, beat the onion, baking powder, salt and pepper.
Squeeze moisture from the shredded potatoes using paper towel.
Add potatoes to the egg mixture.
Stir in the flour.
Pour the oil into a pan over medium heat.
Cook a small amount of the batter for 3 to 4 minutes per side.
Repeat until the rest of the batter is used.
Garnish with the chives.
Nutrition: Calories: 266 Total fat: 11.6g Saturated fat: 2g Cholesterol: 93mg Sodium: 360mg Potassium: 752mg Carbohydrates: 34.6g Fiber: 9g Sugar: 3g Protein: 7.5g

Broccoli Rabe

Preparation Time: 15 minutes
Cooking Time: 15 minutes
Servings: 8
Ingredients:
2 oranges, sliced in half
1 lb. broccoli rabe
2 tablespoons sesame oil, toasted
Salt and pepper to taste
1 tablespoon sesame seeds, toasted

Direction
Pour the oil into a pan over medium heat.
Add the oranges and cook until caramelized.
Transfer to a plate.
Put the broccoli in the pan and cook for 8 minutes.
Squeeze the oranges to release juice in a bowl.
Stir in the oil, salt and pepper.
Coat the broccoli rabe with the mixture.
Sprinkle seeds on top.
Nutrition: Calories: 59 Total fat: 4.4g Saturated fat: 0.6g Sodium: 164mg Potassium: 160mg Carbohydrates: 4.1g Fiber: 1.6g Sugar: 2g Protein: 2.2g

Whipped Potatoes

Preparation Time: 20 minutes
Cooking Time: 35 minutes
Servings: 10
Ingredients:
4 cups water
3 lb. potatoes, sliced into cubes
3 cloves garlic, crushed
6 tablespoons vegan butter
2 bay leaves
10 sage leaves
½ cup Vegan yogurt
¼ cup low-fat milk

Salt to taste
Direction
Boil the potatoes in water for 30 minutes or until tender.
Drain.
In a pan over medium heat, cook the garlic in butter for 1 minute.
Add the sage and cook for 5 more minutes.
Discard the garlic.
Use a fork to mash the potatoes.
Whip using an electric mixer while gradually adding the butter, yogurt, and milk.
Season with salt.
Nutrition: Calories: 169 Total fat: 7.6g Saturated fat: 4.7g Cholesterol: 21mg Sodium: 251mg Potassium: 519mg Carbohydrates: 22.1g Fiber: 1.5g Sugar: 2g Protein: 4.2g

Quinoa Avocado Salad

Preparation Time: 15 minutes
Cooking Time: 4 minutes
Servings: 4
Ingredients:
2 tablespoons balsamic vinegar
¼ cup cream
¼ cup buttermilk
5 tablespoons freshly squeezed lemon juice, divided
1 clove garlic, grated
2 tablespoons shallot, minced
Salt and pepper to taste
2 tablespoons avocado oil, divided
1 ¼ cups quinoa, cooked
2 heads endive, sliced
2 firm pears, sliced thinly
2 avocados, sliced
¼ cup fresh dill, chopped
Direction
Combine the vinegar, cream, milk, 1 tablespoon lemon juice, garlic, shallot, salt and pepper in a bowl.

Pour 1 tablespoon oil into a pan over medium heat.

Heat the quinoa for 4 minutes.

Transfer quinoa to a plate.

Toss the endive and pears in a mixture of remaining oil, remaining lemon juice, salt and pepper.

Transfer to a plate.

Toss the avocado in the reserved dressing.

Add to the plate.

Top with the dill and quinoa.

Nutrition: Calories: 431 Total fat: 28.5g Saturated fat: 8g Cholesterol: 13mg Sodium: 345mg Potassium: 779mg Carbohydrates: 42.7g Fiber: 6g Sugar: 3g Protein: 6.6g

Roasted Sweet Potatoes

Preparation Time: 20 minutes
Cooking Time: 20 minutes
Servings: 4
Ingredients:
2 potatoes, sliced into wedges
2 tablespoons olive oil, divided
Salt and pepper to taste
1 red bell pepper, chopped
¼ cup fresh cilantro, chopped
1 garlic, minced
2 tablespoons almonds, toasted and sliced
1 tablespoon lime juice
Direction
Preheat your oven to 425 degrees F.

Toss the sweet potatoes in oil and salt.

Transfer to a baking pan.

Roast for 20 minutes.

In a bowl, combine the red bell pepper, cilantro, garlic and almonds.

In another bowl, mix the lime juice, remaining oil, salt and pepper.

Drizzle this mixture over the red bell pepper mixture.

Serve sweet potatoes with the red bell pepper mixture.

Nutrition: Calories: 146 Total fat: 8.6g Saturated fat: 1.1g Sodium: 317mg Potassium: 380mg Carbohydrates: 16g Fiber: 2.9g Sugar: 5g Protein: 2.3g

Cauliflower Salad

Preparation Time: 20 minutes
Cooking Time: 15 minutes
Servings: 4
Ingredients:

8 cups cauliflower florets
5 tablespoons olive oil, divided
Salt and pepper to taste
1 cup parsley
1 clove garlic, minced
2 tablespoons lemon juice
¼ cup almonds, toasted and sliced
3 cups arugula
2 tablespoons olives, sliced
¼ cup feta, crumbled
Direction
Preheat your oven to 425 degrees F.

Toss the cauliflower in a mixture of 1 tablespoon olive oil, salt and pepper.

Place in a baking pan and roast for 15 minutes.

Put the parsley, remaining oil, garlic, lemon juice, salt and pepper in a blender.

Pulse until smooth.

Place the roasted cauliflower in a salad bowl.

Stir in the rest of the ingredients along with the parsley dressing.

Nutrition: Calories: 198 Total fat: 16.5g Saturated fat: 3g Cholesterol: 6mg Sodium: 3mg Potassium: 570mg Carbohydrates: 10.4g Fiber: 4.1g Sugar: 4g Protein: 5.4g

Garlic Mashed Potatoes & Turnips

Preparation Time: 20 minutes
Cooking Time: 30 minutes
Servings: 8
Ingredients:
1 head garlic
1 teaspoon olive oil
1 lb. turnips, sliced into cubes
2 lb. potatoes, sliced into cubes
½ cup almond milk
½ cup vegan parmesan cheese, grated
1 tablespoon fresh thyme, chopped
1 tablespoon fresh chives, chopped
2 tablespoons vegan butter
Salt and pepper to taste
Direction
Preheat your oven to 375 degrees F.

Slice the tip off the garlic head.

Drizzle with a little oil and roast in the oven for 45 minutes.

Boil the turnips and potatoes in a pot of water for 30 minutes or until tender.

Add all the ingredients to a food processor along with the garlic.

Pulse until smooth.

Nutrition: Calories: 141 Total fat: 3.2g Saturated fat: 1.5g Cholesterol: 7mg Sodium: 284mg Potassium: 676mg Carbohydrates: 24.6g Fiber: 3.1g Sugar: 4g Protein: 4.6g

Green Beans with vegan Bacon

Preparation Time: 15 minutes
Cooking Time: 20 minutes
Servings: 8
Ingredients:
2 slices of vegan bacon, chopped
1 shallot, chopped
24 oz. green beans
Salt and pepper to taste
½ teaspoon smoked paprika
1 teaspoon lemon juice
2 teaspoons vinegar
Direction
Preheat your oven to 450 degrees F.

Add the bacon in the baking pan and roast for 5 minutes.

Stir in the shallot and beans.

Season with salt, pepper and paprika.

Roast for 10 minutes.

Drizzle with the lemon juice and vinegar.

Roast for another 2 minutes.

Nutrition: Calories: 49 Total fat: 1.2g Saturated fat: 0.4g Cholesterol: 3mg Sodium: 192mg Potassium: 249mg Carbohydrates: 8.1g Fiber: 3g Sugar: 4g Protein: 2.9g

Coconut Brussels Sprouts

Preparation Time: 15 minutes
Cooking Time: 10 minutes
Servings: 4
Ingredients:
1 lb. Brussels sprouts, trimmed and sliced in half
2 tablespoons coconut oil
¼ cup coconut water
1 tablespoon soy sauce
Direction
In a pan over medium heat, add the coconut oil and cook the Brussels sprouts for 4 minutes.

Pour in the coconut water.

Cook for 3 minutes.

Add the soy sauce and cook for another 1 minute.

Nutrition: Calories: 114 Total fat: 7.1g Saturated fat: 5.7g Sodium: 269mg Potassium: 483mg Carbohydrates: 11.1g Fiber: 4.3g Sugar: 3g Protein: 4g

Cod Stew with Rice & Sweet Potatoes

Preparation Time: 30 minutes
Cooking Time: 1 hour
Servings: 4
Ingredients:
2 cups water
¾ cup brown rice
1 tablespoon vegetable oil
1 tablespoon ginger, chopped
1 tablespoon garlic, chopped
1 sweet potato, sliced into cubes
1 bell pepper, sliced
1 tablespoon curry powder
Salt to taste
15 oz. coconut milk
4 cod fillets
2 teaspoons freshly squeezed lime juice
3 tablespoons cilantro, chopped
Direction
Place the water and rice in a saucepan.

Bring to a boil and then simmer for 30 to 40 minutes. Set aside.

Pour the oil in a pan over medium heat.

Cook the garlic for 30 seconds.

Add the sweet potatoes and bell pepper.

Season with curry powder and salt.

Mix well.

Pour in the coconut milk.

Simmer for 15 minutes.

Nestle the fish into the sauce and cook for another 10 minutes.

Stir in the lime juice and cilantro.

Serve with the rice.

Nutrition: Calories: 382 Total fat: 11.3g Saturated fat: 4.8g Cholesterol: 45mg Sodium: 413mg Potassium: 736mg Carbohydrates: 49.5g Fiber: 5.3g Sugar: 8g Protein: 19.2g

Vegan Chicken & Rice

Preparation Time: 15 minutes
Cooking Time: 3 hours and 30 minutes
Servings: 8
Ingredients:
8 Tofu thighs
Salt and pepper to taste
½ teaspoon ground coriander
2 teaspoons ground cumin
17 oz. brown rice, cooked
30 oz. black beans
1 tablespoon olive oil
Pinch cayenne pepper
2 cups pico de gallo
¾ cup radish, sliced thinly
2 avocados, sliced
Direction
Season the tofu with salt, pepper, coriander and cumin.
Place in a slow cooker.
Pour in the stock.
Cook on low for 3 hours and 30 minutes.
Place the tofu in a cutting board.
Shred the chicken.
Toss the tofu shreds in the cooking liquid.
Serve the rice in bowls, topped with the tofu and the rest of the ingredients.
Nutrition: Calories: 470 Total fat: 17g Saturated fat: 3g Sodium: 615mg Carbohydrates: 40g Fiber: 11g Sugar: 1g Protein: 40g

Rice Bowl with Edamame

Preparation Time: 10 minutes
Cooking Time: 3 hours and 50 minutes
Servings: 6
Ingredients:
1 tablespoon coconut oil, melted
¾ cup brown rice (uncooked)
1 cup wild rice (uncooked)
Cooking spray
4 cups vegetable stock
8 oz. shelled edamame
1 onion, chopped
Salt to taste
½ cup dried cherries, sliced
½ cup pecans, toasted and sliced
1 tablespoon red wine vinegar

Direction
Add the rice and coconut oil in a slow cooker sprayed with oil.
Pour in the stock and stir in the edamame and onions.
Season with salt.
Seal the pot.
Cook on high for 3 hours and 30 minutes.
Stir in the dried cherries.
Let sit for 5 minutes.
Stir in the rest of the ingredients before serving.
Nutrition: Calories: 381 Total fat: 12g 18 % Saturated fat: 2g Sodium: 459mg Carbohydrates: 61g Fiber: 7g Sugar: 13g Protein: 12g

Chickpea Avocado Sandwich

You can make the chickpea and avocado filling ahead of time and store it in the cold-storage box for or in the icebox. While avocado does brown easily, the lime juice helps preserve the integrity of it.
Preparation time: 10 minutes
Cooking Time: 5 minutes
Servings: 2
Ingredients:
Chickpeas – 1 can
Avocado – 1
Dill, dried – .25 teaspoon
Onion powder – .25 teaspoon
Sea salt – .5 teaspoon
Celery, chopped – .25 cup
Green onion, chopped – .25 cup
Lime juice – 3 tablespoons
Garlic powder – .5 teaspoon
Dark pepper, ground – dash
Tomato, sliced – 1

Lettuce – 4 leaves
Bread – 4 slices
Directions:
Drain the canned chickpeas and rinse them under cool water. Place them in a bowl along with the herbs, spices, sea salt, avocado, and lime juice. Using a potato masher or fork, mash the avocado and chickpeas together until you have a thick filling. Try not to mash the chickpeas all the way, as they create texture.

Stir the celery and green onion into the filling and prepare your sandwiches.

Layout two slices of bread, top them with the chickpea filling, some lettuce, and sliced tomato. Top them off with the two remaining slices, slice the sandwiches in half, and serve.

Nutrition: Calories 471

Roasted Tomato Sandwich

This sandwich is full of fresh ingredients, many of which cannot be prepared ahead. But, when you simply have to prepare some lettuce, an avocado, or tomato, this is not a problem. You can still have an easy and quick meal. But, that doesn't mean you can't prepare any aspects of this sandwich ahead of time. If using homemade bread, you can prepare it at the beginning of the week and store it in the cold-storage box or icebox. You can also prepare the garlic aioli ahead of time and store it in a Mason jar in the fridge.

Preparation time: 30 minutes
Cooking Time: 25 minutes
Servings: 2
Ingredients:
Sourdough bread – 4 slices
Tomatoes, large, cut into eight rounds – 2
Avocado – 1
Sea salt – .25 teaspoon
Vegan mayonnaise – .25 cup
Garlic, minced – 2 cloves
Juice of lemon fruit – 1 tablespoon
Oregano, dried – .25 teaspoon
Black ground pepper – .25 teaspoon
Olive oil – 2 tablespoons
Fresh basil – .25 cup
Arugula – .25 cup
Directions:
Begin by setting your electric cooker to Fahrenheit 350 degrees and lining an aluminum sheet pan with kitchen parchment. Layout the sliced tomatoes on the sheet, and sprinkle them with part of the salt, oregano, and pepper, and

allow them to roast until tender, about fifteen minutes.

Meanwhile, prepare the garlic aioli. Whisk together the mayonnaise, garlic, juice of lemon fruit, and some sea salt and pepper. Chill in the fridge until use.

Use a pastry brush and coat one side of each slice of bread with the olive oil. While doing this preheat a skillet over midway warmth. Once hot, toast the bread oil-side down until browned and then remove them from the heat.

To prepare the sandwiches, lay out the bread, oil side down. On each slice spread the garlic aioli. On half of the slices cover with the roasted tomatoes, sliced avocado, basil, and arugula. Top these slices with their matched slice without toppings. Slice the sandwiches in half before serving.

Nutrition: Calories 525

Pulled "Pork" Sandwiches

This pulled "pork" is the perfect dish to make ahead. Prepare the mushrooms and coat them in the sauce and then you can store them chilled in the cold-storage box or the icebox. If you prepare a large amount to keep in the icebox, you will always have some on hand for sandwiches, pizza, nachos, or any other vegan-version of popular dishes that might be complemented by pulled "pork".

Preparation time: 40 minutes
Cooking Time: 35 minutes
Servings: 3
Ingredients:
King oyster mushrooms* – 4
Barbecue sauce – .25 cup
Olive oil – 2 tablespoons
Sea salt – .25 teaspoon
Garlic, minced – 2 cloves
Cayenne pepper – .25 teaspoon
Bread – 6 slices

Directions:

Start by setting your electric cooker to Fahrenheit 400 degrees.

While your electric cooker warms up, clean the mushrooms with a damp paper towel and then use two forks to shred both the caps and stems of the mushrooms into pieces resembling pulled pork. Place the shredded mushrooms on a kitchen parchment-lined aluminum baking sheet.

Drizzle the mushrooms with half of the olive oil and then toss them with the seasoning and garlic until evenly coated. Allow the oyster mushrooms to roast until slightly crispy and browned about twenty minutes.

In a skillet, add the remaining tablespoon of olive oil, allowing it to warm over midway-elevated. Put the cooked mushrooms in the pan along with the barbecue sauce.

Cook the mushrooms in the sauce while stirring until the sauce is fragrant and warm, about three to five minutes. Top three slices of bread with this concoction and top with the remaining three slices. Cut the sandwiches in half before serving.

Note:

*If you can't find king oyster mushrooms, then you can use three heaping cups of regular oyster mushrooms.

Nutrition: Calories 259

Noodles Alfredo with Herby Tofu

Preparation Time: 10 minutes
Cooking Time: 5 minutes
Servings: 4
Ingredients:
2 tbsp vegetable oil
2 (14 oz.) blocks extra-firm tofu, pressed and cubed
12 ounces eggless noodles
1 tbsp dried mixed herbs

2 cups cashews, soaked overnight and drained
¾ cups unsweetened almond milk
½ cup nutritional yeast
4 garlic cloves, roasted (roasting is optional but highly recommended)
½ cup onion, coarsely chopped
1 lemon, juiced
½ cup sun-dried tomatoes
Salt and black pepper to taste
2 tbsp chopped fresh basil leaves to garnish
Directions:

Heat the vegetable oil in a large skillet over medium heat.

Season the tofu with the mixed herbs, salt, black pepper, and fry in the oil until golden brown. Transfer to a paper-towel-lined plate and set aside. Turn the heat off.

In a blender, combine the almond milk, nutritional yeast, garlic, onion, and lemon juice. Set aside.

Reheat the vegetable oil in the skillet over medium heat and sauté the noodles for 2 minutes. Stir in the sundried tomatoes and the cashew (Alfredo) sauce. Reduce the heat to low and cook for 2 more minutes.

If the sauce is too thick, thin with some more almond milk to your desired thickness.

Dish the food, garnish with the basil and serve warm.

Lemon Couscous with Tempeh Kabobs

Preparation Time: 2 hours 15 minutes
Cooking Time: 2 hours
Servings: 4
Ingredients:
For the tempeh kabobs:
1 ½ cups of water
10 oz. tempeh, cut into 1-inch chunks
1 red onion, cut into 1-inch chunks
1 small yellow squash, cut into 1-inch chunks
1 small green squash, cut into 1-inch chunks
2 tbsp. olive oil
1 cup sugar-free barbecue sauce
8 wooden skewers, soaked
For the lemon couscous:
1 ½ cups whole wheat couscous
2 cups of water
Salt to taste
¼ cup chopped parsley
¼ chopped mint leaves
¼ cup chopped cilantro
1 lemon, juiced

1 medium avocado, pitted, sliced and peeled

Directions:

For the tempeh kabobs:

Boil the water in a medium pot over medium heat.

Once boiled, turn the heat off, and put the tempeh in it. Cover the lid and let the tempeh steam for 5 minutes (this is to remove its bitterness). Drain the tempeh after.

After, pour the barbecue sauce into a medium bowl, add the tempeh, and coat well with the sauce. Cover the bowl with plastic wrap and marinate for 2 hours.

After 2 hours, preheat a grill to 350 F.

On the skewers, alternately thread single chunks of the tempeh, onion, yellow squash, and green squash until the ingredients are exhausted.

Lightly grease the grill grates with olive oil, place the skewers on top and brush with some barbecue sauce. Cook for 3 minutes on each side while brushing with more barbecue sauce as you turn the kabobs.

Transfer to a plate for serving.

For the lemon couscous:

Meanwhile, as the kabobs cooked, pour the couscous, water, and salt into a medium bowl and steam in the microwave for 3 to 4 minutes. Remove the bowl from the microwave and allow slight cooling.

Stir in the parsley, mint leaves, cilantro, and lemon juice.

Garnish the couscous with the avocado slices and serve with the tempeh kabobs.

Portobello Burger with Veggie Fries

Preparation Time: 45 minutes
Cooking Time: 30 minutes
Servings: 4
Ingredients:
For the veggie fries:

3 carrots, peeled and julienned
2 sweet potatoes, peeled and julienned
1 rutabaga, peeled and julienned
2 tsp olive oil
¼ tsp paprika
Salt and black pepper to taste
For the Portobello burgers:
1 clove garlic, minced
½ tsp salt
2 tbsp. olive oil
4 whole-wheat buns
4 Portobello mushroom caps
½ cup sliced roasted red peppers
2 tbsp. pitted Kalamata olives, chopped
2 medium tomatoes, chopped
½ tsp dried oregano
¼ cup crumbled feta cheese (optional)
1 tbsp. red wine vinegar
2 cups baby salad greens
½ cup hummus for serving
Directions:
For the veggie fries:
Preheat the oven to 400 F.

Spread the carrots, sweet potatoes, and rutabaga on a baking sheet and season with the olive oil, paprika, salt, and black pepper. Use your hands to rub the seasoning well onto the vegetables. Bake in the oven for 20 minutes or until the vegetables soften (stir halfway).

When ready, transfer to a plate and use it for serving.

For the Portobello burgers:

Meanwhile, as the vegetable roast, heat a grill pan over medium heat.

Use a spoon to crush the garlic with salt in a bowl. Stir in 1 tablespoon of the olive oil.

Brush the mushrooms on both sides with the garlic mixture and grill in the pan on both sides until tender, 8 minutes. Transfer to a plate and set aside.

Toast the buns in the pan until crispy, 2 minutes. Set aside in a plate.

In a bowl, combine the remaining ingredients except for the hummus and divide on the bottom parts of the buns.

Top with the hummus, cover the burger with the top parts of the buns and serve with the veggie fries.

Thai Seitan Vegetable Curry

Preparation Time: 20 minutes
Cooking Time: 15 minutes
Servings: 4

Ingredients:
1 tbsp vegetable oil
4 cups diced seitan
1 cup sliced mixed bell peppers
½ cup onions diced
1 small head broccoli, cut into florets
2 tbsp Thai red curry paste
1 tsp garlic puree
1 cup unsweetened coconut milk
2 tbsp vegetable broth
2 cups spinach
Salt and black pepper to taste
Directions:
Heat the vegetable oil in a large skillet over medium heat and fry the seitan until slightly dark brown. Mix in the bell peppers, onions, broccoli, and cook until softened, 4 minutes.

Mix the curry paste, garlic puree, and 1 tablespoon of coconut milk. Cook for 1 minute and stir in the remaining coconut milk and vegetable broth. Simmer for 10 minutes.

Stir in the spinach to wilt and season the curry with salt and black pepper.

Serve the curry with steamed white or brown rice.

Tofu Cabbage Stir-Fry

Preparation Time: 15 minutes
Cooking Time: 10 minutes
Servings: 4
Ingredients:
5 oz. vegan butter
2 ½ cups baby bok choy, quartered lengthwise
8 oz sliced mushrooms
2 cups extra-firm tofu, pressed and cubed
Salt and black pepper to taste
1 tsp onion powder
1 tsp garlic powder
1 tbsp plain vinegar
2 garlic cloves, minced
1 tsp chili flakes
1 tbsp fresh ginger, grated
3 scallions, sliced
1 tbsp sesame oil
1 cup vegan mayonnaise
Wasabi paste to taste
Cooked white or brown rice (1/2 cup per person)

Directions:
Melt half of the vegan butter in a wok and sauté the bok choy until softened, 3 minutes.

Season with salt, black pepper, onion powder, garlic powder, and vinegar. Sauté for 2 minutes to combine the flavors and plate the bok choy.

Melt the remaining vegan butter in the wok and sauté the garlic, mushrooms, chili flakes, and ginger until fragrant.

Stir in the tofu and cook until browned on all sides. Add the scallions and bok choy, heat for 2 minutes and drizzle in the sesame oil.

In a small bowl, mix the vegan mayonnaise and wasabi, and mix into the tofu and vegetables. Cook for 2 minutes and dish the food.

Serve warm with steamed rice.

Curried Tofu with Buttery Cabbage

Preparation Time: 15 minutes
Cooking Time: 10 minutes
Servings: 4
Ingredients:
2 cups extra-firm tofu, pressed and cubed
1 tbsp + 3 ½ tbsp coconut oil
½ cup unsweetened shredded coconut
1 tsp yellow curry powder
1 tsp salt
½ tsp onion powder
2 cups Napa cabbage
4 oz. vegan butter
Salt and black pepper to taste
Lemon wedges for serving
Directions:
In a medium bowl, add the tofu, 1 tablespoon of coconut oil, curry powder, salt, and onion powder. Mix well until the tofu is well-coated with the spices.

Heat the remaining coconut oil in a non-stick skillet and fry the tofu until golden brown on all sides, 8 minutes. Divide onto serving plates and set aside for serving.

In another skillet, melt half of the vegan butter, and sauté the cabbage until slightly caramelized, 2 minutes. Season with salt, black pepper, and plate to the side of the tofu.

Melt the remaining vegan butter in the skillet and drizzle all over the cabbage.

Serve warm.

Smoked Tempeh with Broccoli Fritters

Preparation Time: 25 minutes
Cooking Time: 20 minutes
Servings: 4
Ingredients:
For the flax egg:
4 tbsp flax seed powder + 12 tbsp water
For the grilled tempeh:
3 tbsp olive oil
1 tbsp soy sauce
3 tbsp fresh lime juice
1 tbsp grated ginger
Salt and cayenne pepper to taste
10 oz. tempeh slices
For the broccoli fritters:
2 cups of rice broccoli
8 oz. tofu cheese
3 tbsp plain flour
½ tsp onion powder
1 tsp salt
¼ tsp freshly ground black pepper
4¼ oz. vegan butter
For serving:
½ cup mixed salad greens
1 cup vegan mayonnaise
½ lemon, juiced
Directions:
For the smoked tempeh:
In a bowl, mix the flax seed powder with water and set aside to soak for 5 minutes.

In another bowl, combine the olive oil, soy sauce, lime juice, grated ginger, salt, and cayenne pepper. Brush the tempeh slices with the mixture.

Heat a grill pan over medium heat and grill the tempeh on both sides until nicely smoked and golden brown, 8 minutes. Transfer to a plate and set aside in a warmer for serving.

In a medium bowl, combine the broccoli rice, tofu cheese, flour, onion, salt, and black pepper. Mix in the flax egg until well combine and form 1-inch thick patties out of the mixture.

Melt the vegan butter in a medium skillet over medium heat and fry the patties on both sides until golden brown, 8 minutes. Remove the fritters onto a plate and set aside.

In a small bowl, mix the vegan mayonnaise with the lemon juice.

Divide the smoked tempeh and broccoli fritters onto serving plates, add the salad greens, and serve with the vegan mayonnaise sauce.

Cheesy Potato Casserole

Preparation Time: 30 minutes
Cooking Time: 20 minutes
Servings: 4
Ingredients:
2 oz. vegan butter
½ cup celery stalks, finely chopped
1 white onion, finely chopped
1 green bell pepper, seeded and finely chopped
Salt and black pepper to taste
2 cups peeled and chopped potatoes
1 cup vegan mayonnaise
4 oz. freshly shredded vegan Parmesan cheese
1 tsp red chili flakes
Directions:
Preheat the oven to 400 F and grease a baking dish with cooking spray.

Season the celery, onion, and bell pepper with salt and black pepper.

In a bowl, mix the potatoes, vegan mayonnaise, Parmesan cheese, and red chili flakes.

Pour the mixture into the baking dish, add the season vegetables, and mix well.

Bake in the oven until golden brown, about 20 minutes.

Remove the baked potato and serve warm with baby spinach.

Curry Mushroom Pie

Preparation Time: 65 minutes
Cooking Time: 1 hour
Servings: 4
Ingredients:
For the piecrust:
1 tbsp flax seed powder + 3 tbsp water
¾ cup plain flour
4 tbsp. chia seeds
4 tbsp almond flour
1 tbsp nutritional yeast
1 tsp baking powder
1 pinch salt

3 tbsp olive oil
4 tbsp water
For the filling:
1 cup chopped baby Bella mushrooms
1 cup vegan mayonnaise
3 tbsp + 9 tbsp water
½ red bell pepper, finely chopped
1 tsp curry powder
½ tsp paprika powder
½ tsp garlic powder
¼ tsp black pepper
½ cup coconut cream
1¼ cups shredded vegan Parmesan cheese

Directions:

In two separate bowls, mix the different portions of flaxseed powder with the respective quantity of water. Allow soaking for 5 minutes.

For the piecrust:

Preheat the oven to 350 F.

When the flax egg is ready, pour the smaller quantity into a food processor and pour in all the ingredients for the piecrust. Blend until soft, smooth dough forms.

Line an 8-inch springform pan with parchment paper and grease with cooking spray.

Spread the dough in the bottom of the pan and bake for 15 minutes.

For the filling:

In a bowl, add the remaining flax egg and all the filling's ingredients. Combine well and pour the mixture on the piecrust. Bake further for 40 minutes or until the pie is golden brown.

Remove from the oven and allow cooling for 1 minute.

Slice and serve the pie warm.

Spicy Cheesy Tofu Balls

Preparation Time: 30 minutes
Cooking Time: 15 minutes
Servings: 4
Ingredients:
⅓ cup vegan mayonnaise
¼ cup pickled jalapenos
1 pinch cayenne pepper
4 oz. grated vegan cheddar cheese
1 tsp paprika powder
1 tbsp mustard powder
1 tbsp flax seed powder + 3 tbsp water
2 ½ cup crumbled tofu
Salt and black pepper to taste
2 tbsp vegan butter, for frying
Directions:
For the spicy cheese:

In a bowl, mix all the ingredients for the spicy vegan cheese until well combined. Set aside.

In another medium bowl, combine the flax seed powder with water and allow soaking for 5 minutes.

Add the flax egg to the cheese mixture, the crumbled tofu, salt, and black pepper, and combine well. Use your hands to form large meatballs out of the mix.

Melt the vegan butter in a large skillet over medium heat and fry the tofu balls until cooked and golden brown on all sides, 10 minutes.

Serve the tofu balls with your favorite mashes or in burgers.

Radish Chips

Preparation Time: 20 Minutes
Cooking Time: 10 Minutes
Servings: 4
Ingredients:
10-15 Radishes, Large
Sea Salt & Black Pepper to Taste
Directions:
Start by heating your oven to 375.

Slice your radishes thin, and then spread them out on a cookie sheet that's been sprayed with cooking spray.

Mist the radishes with cooking spray, and then season with salt and pepper.

Bake for ten minutes, and then flip.

Bake for five to ten minutes more. They should be crispy.

Interesting Facts: Potatoes are a great starchy source of potassium and protein. They are pretty inexpensive if you are one that is watching their budget. Bonus: Very heart healthy!

Sautéed Pears

Preparation Time: 35 Minutes
Cooking Time: 30 Minutes
Servings: 6
Ingredients:
2 Tablespoons Margarine (Or Vegan Butter)
¼ Teaspoon Cinnamon
¼ Teaspoon Nutmeg
6 Bosc Pears, Peeled & Quartered
1 Tablespoon Lemon Juice
½ Cup Walnuts, Toasted & Chopped (Optional)
Directions:
Melt your vegan butter in a skillet, and then add your spices. Cook for a half a minute before adding in your pears.

Cook for fifteen minutes, and then stir in your lemon juice.

Serve with walnuts if desired.

Interesting Facts: Cinnamon: This spice is an absolute powerhouse and is considered one of the healthiest, beneficial spices on the plant. It's widely known for its medicinal properties. This spice is loaded with powerful antioxidants and is popular for its anti-inflammatory properties. It can reduce heart disease and lower blood sugar levels.

Pecan & Blueberry Crumble

Preparation Time: 40 Minutes
Cooking Time: 1 Hour
Servings: 6
Calories: 381
Protein: 10 Grams
Fat: 32 Grams
Net Carbs: 20 Grams
Ingredients:
14 Ounces Blueberries
1 Tablespoon Lemon Juice, Fresh
1 ½ Teaspoon Stevia Powder
3 Tablespoons Chia Seeds
2 Cups Almond Flour, Blanched
¼ Cup Pecans, Chopped
5 Tablespoon coconut Oil
2 Tablespoon Cinnamon
Directions:
Mix together your blueberries, stevia, chia seeds and lemon juice, and place it in an iron skillet.

Mix ingredients while spreading it over your blueberries.

Heat your oven to 400, and then transfer it to an oven safe skillet, baking for a half hour.

Interesting Facts: Blueberries: These guys are a delectable treat that is easily incorporated into many dishes. They are packed with antioxidants and Vitamin C. Bonus: Blueberries have been proven to promote eye health and slow macular degeneration.

Rice Pudding

Preparation Time: 1 Hour 35 Minutes
Cooking Time: 1 Hour and 30 Minutes
Servings: 6
Ingredients:
1 Cup Brown Rice
1 Teaspoon Vanilla Extract, Pure
½ Teaspoon Sea Salt, Fine
½ Teaspoon Cinnamon
¼ Teaspoon Nutmeg
3 Egg Substitutes
3 Cups Coconut Milk, Light
2 Cups Brown Rice, Cooked

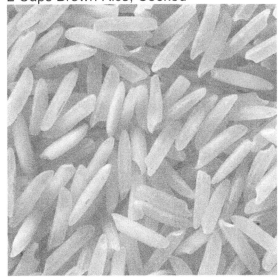

Directions:
Blend all of your ingredients together before pouring them into a two quarter dish.

Bake at 300 for ninety minutes before serving.

Interesting Facts: Brown rice is incredibly high in antioxidants and good vitamins. It's relative, 14 white rice is far less beneficial as much of these healthy nutrients get destroyed during the process of milling. You can also opt for red and black rice or wild rice. The meal options for this healthy grain are limitless!

Mango Sticky Rice

Preparation Time: 35 Minutes
Cooking Time: 30 Minutes
Servings: 3
Calories: 571
Protein: 6 Grams
Fat: 29.6 Grams
Carbs: 77.6 Grams
Ingredients:
½ Cup Sugar
1 Mango, Sliced
14 Ounces Coconut Milk, Canned
½ Cup Basmati Rice

Directions:
Cook your rice per package instructions, and add half of your sugar. When cooking your rice, substitute half of your water for half of your coconut milk.

Boil your remaining coconut milk in a saucepan with your remaining sugar.

Boil on high heat until it's thick, and then add in your mango slices.

Interesting Facts: Mangos contain 50% of the daily Vitamin C you should consume which aid in bone and immune health.

Smoothies and Beverages

Fruity Smoothie

Preparation Time: 10 Minutes
Cooking time: 0 minute
Servings: 1
Ingredients:
¾ cup soy yogurt
½ cup pineapple juice
1 cup pineapple chunks
1 cup raspberries, sliced
1 cup blueberries, sliced
Direction:
Process the ingredients in a blender.
Chill before serving.
Nutrition: Calories 279, Total Fat 2 g, Saturated Fat 0 g Cholesterol 4 mg, Sodium 149 mg, Total Carbohydrate 56 g   Dietary Fiber 7 g, Protein 12 g, Total Sugars 46 g   Potassium 719 mg

Energizing Ginger Detox Tonic

Preparation time: 15 minutes
Cooking time: 10 minutes
Servings: 2
Ingredients:
1/2 teaspoon of grated ginger, fresh
1 small lemon slice
1/8 teaspoon of cayenne pepper
1/8 teaspoon of ground turmeric
1/8 teaspoon of ground cinnamon
1 teaspoon of maple syrup
1 teaspoon of apple cider vinegar
2 cups of boiling water
Directions:
Pour the boiling water into a small saucepan, add and stir the ginger, then let it rest for 8 to 10 minutes, before covering the pan.
Pass the mixture through a strainer and into the liquid, add the cayenne pepper, turmeric, cinnamon and stir properly.
Add the maple syrup, vinegar, and lemon slice.
Add and stir an infused lemon and serve immediately.
Nutrition: Calories:80 Cal, Carbohydrates:0g, Protein:0g, Fats:0g, Fiber:0g.

Warm Spiced Lemon Drink

Preparation time: 2 hours and 10 minutes
Cooking time: 2 hours
Servings: 12
Ingredients:
1 cinnamon stick, about 3 inches long
1/2 teaspoon of whole cloves
2 cups of coconut sugar
4 fluid of ounce pineapple juice
1/2 cup and 2 tablespoons of lemon juice
12 fluid ounce of orange juice
2 1/2 quarts of water
Directions:
Pour water into a 6-quarts slow cooker and stir the sugar and lemon juice properly.

Wrap the cinnamon, the whole cloves in cheesecloth and tie its corners with string.

Immerse this cheesecloth bag in the liquid present in the slow cooker and cover it with the lid.

Then plug in the slow cooker and let it cook on high heat setting for 2 hours or until it is heated thoroughly.

When done, discard the cheesecloth bag and serve the drink hot or cold.

Nutrition: Calories:15   Cal, Carbohydrates:3.2g,   Protein:0.1g,   Fats:0g, Fiber:0g.

Soothing Ginger Tea Drink

Preparation time: 2 hours and 15 minutes
Cooking time: 2 hours and 10 minutes
Servings: 8
Ingredients:
1 tablespoon of minced ginger root
2 tablespoons of honey
15 green tea bags
32 fluid ounce of white grape juice
2 quarts of boiling water
Directions:
Pour water into a 4-quarts slow cooker, immerse tea bags, cover the cooker and let stand for 10 minutes.

After 10 minutes, remove and discard tea bags and stir in remaining ingredients.

Return cover to slow cooker, then plug in and let cook at high heat setting for 2 hours or until heated through.

When done, strain the liquid and serve hot or cold.

Nutrition: Calories:45   Cal, Carbohydrates:12g,   Protein:0g,   Fats:0g, Fiber:0g.

Nice Spiced Cherry Cider

Preparation time: 4 hours and 5 minutes
Cooking time: 4 hours
Servings: 16
Ingredients:
2 cinnamon sticks, each about 3 inches long
6-ounce of cherry gelatin
4 quarts of apple cider
Directions:
Using a 6-quarts slow cooker, pour the apple cider and add the cinnamon stick.

Stir, then cover the slow cooker with its lid. Plug in the cooker and let it cook for 3 hours at the high heat setting or until it is heated thoroughly.

Then add and stir the gelatin properly, then continue cooking for another hour.

When done, remove the cinnamon sticks and serve the drink hot or cold.

Nutrition: ,   Calories:100   Cal, Carbohydrates:0g, Protein:0g, Fats:0g, Fiber:0g.

Fragrant Spiced Coffee

Preparation time: 3 hours and 10 minutes
Cooking time: 3 hours
Servings: 8
Ingredients:
4 cinnamon sticks, each about 3 inches long
1 1/2 teaspoons of whole cloves
1/3 cup of honey
2-ounce of chocolate syrup
1/2 teaspoon of anise extract
8 cups of brewed coffee

Directions:
Pour the coffee in a 4-quarts slow cooker and pour in the remaining ingredients except for cinnamon and stir properly.

Wrap the whole cloves in cheesecloth and tie its corners with strings.

Immerse this cheesecloth bag in the liquid present in the slow cooker and cover it with the lid.

Then plug in the slow cooker and let it cook on the low heat setting for 3 hours or until heated thoroughly.

When done, discard the cheesecloth bag and serve.

Nutrition: Calories:150 Cal, Carbohydrates:35g, Protein:3g, Fats:0g, Fiber:0g.

Tangy Spiced Cranberry Drink

Preparation time: 3 hours and 10 minutes
Cooking time: 3 hours
Servings: 14
Ingredients:
1 1/2 cups of coconut sugar
12 whole cloves
2 fluid ounce of lemon juice
6 fluid ounce of orange juice
32 fluid ounce of cranberry juice
8 cups of hot water
1/2 cup of Red Hot candies
Directions:
Pour the water into a 6-quarts slow cooker along with the cranberry juice, orange juice, and the lemon juice.

Stir the sugar properly.

Wrap the whole cloves in a cheese cloth, tie its corners with strings, and immerse it in the liquid present inside the slow cooker.

Add the red hot candies to the slow cooker and cover it with the lid.

Then plug in the slow cooker and let it cook on the low heat setting for 3 hours or until it is heated thoroughly.

When done, discard the cheesecloth bag and serve.

Nutrition: Calories:89 Cal, Carbohydrates:27g, Protein:0g, Fats:0g, Fiber:1g.

Warm Pomegranate Punch

Preparation time: 3 hours and 15 minutes
Cooking time: 3 hours
Servings: 10
Ingredients:
3 cinnamon sticks, each about 3 inches long
12 whole cloves
1/2 cup of coconut sugar
1/3 cup of lemon juice
32 fluid ounce of pomegranate juice
32 fluid ounce of apple juice, unsweetened
16 fluid ounce of brewed tea

Directions:
Using a 4-quart slow cooker, pour the lemon juice, pomegranate, juice apple juice, tea, and then sugar.

Wrap the whole cloves and cinnamon stick in a cheese cloth, tie its corners with a string, and immerse it in the liquid present in the slow cooker.

Then cover it with the lid, plug in the slow cooker and let it cook at the low heat setting for 3 hours or until it is heated thoroughly.

When done, discard the cheesecloth bag and serve it hot or cold.

Nutrition: Calories:253 Cal, Carbohydrates:58g, Protein:7g, Fats:2g, Fiber:3g.

Rich Truffle Hot Chocolate

Preparation time: 2 hours and 10 minutes
Cooking time: 2 hours
Servings: 4
Ingredients:
1/3 cup of cocoa powder, unsweetened
1/3 cup of coconut sugar
1/8 teaspoon of salt
1/8 teaspoon of ground cinnamon
1 teaspoon of vanilla extract, unsweetened
32 fluid ounce of coconut milk

Directions:

Using a 2 quarts slow cooker, add all the ingredients and stir properly.

Cover it with the lid, then plug in the slow cooker and cook it for 2 hours on the high heat setting or until it is heated thoroughly.

When done, serve right away.

Nutrition: Calories:67 Cal, Carbohydrates:13g, Protein:2g, Fats:2g, Fiber:2.3g.

Ultimate Mulled Wine

Preparation time: 35 minutes
Cooking time: 30 minutes
Servings: 6
Ingredients:
1 cup of cranberries, fresh
2 oranges, juiced
1 tablespoon of whole cloves
2 cinnamon sticks, each about 3 inches long
1 tablespoon of star anise
1/3 cup of honey
8 fluid ounce of apple cider
8 fluid ounce of cranberry juice
24 fluid ounce of red wine
Directions:

Using a 4 quarts slow cooker, add all the ingredients and stir properly.

Cover it with the lid, then plug in the slow cooker and cook it for 30 minutes on thee high heat setting or until it gets warm thoroughly.

When done, strain the wine and serve right away.

Nutrition: Calories:202 Cal, Carbohydrates:25g, Protein:0g, Fats:0g, Fiber:0g.

Pleasant Lemonade

Preparation time: 3 hours and 15 minutes
Cooking time: 3 hours
Servings: 10 servings
Ingredients:
Cinnamon sticks for serving
2 cups of coconut sugar
1/4 cup of honey
3 cups of lemon juice. fresh
32 fluid ounce of water
Directions:

Using a 4-quarts slow cooker, place all the ingredients except for the cinnamon sticks and stir properly.

Cover it with the lid, then plug in the slow cooker and cook it for 3 hours on the low heat setting or until it is heated thoroughly.

When done, stir properly and serve with the cinnamon sticks.

Nutrition: Calories:146 Cal, Carbohydrates:34g, Protein:0g, Fats:0g, Fiber:0g.

Pineapple, Banana & Spinach Smoothie

Preparation Time: 10 Minutes
Cooking time: 0 minute
Servings: 1
Ingredients:
½ cup almond milk
¼ cup soy yogurt
1 cup spinach
1 cup banana
1 cup pineapple chunks
1 tbsp. chia seeds
Direction:

Add all the ingredients in a blender.
Blend until smooth.
Chill in the refrigerator before serving.
Nutrition: Calories 297, Total Fat 6 g, Saturated Fat 1 g, Cholesterol 4 mg Sodium 145 mg, Total Carbohydrate 54 g, Dietary Fiber 10 g Protein 13 g, Total Sugars 29g, Potassium 1038 mg

Kale & Avocado Smoothie

Preparation Time: 10 Minutes
Cooking time: 0 minute
Servings: 1
Ingredients:
1 ripe banana
1 cup kale
1 cup almond milk
¼ avocado
1 tbsp. chia seeds
2 tsp. honey
1 cup ice cubes
Direction:
Blend all the ingredients until smooth.
Nutrition: Calories 343   Total Fat 14 g Saturated Fat 2 g Cholesterol 0 mg Sodium 199 mg Total Carbohydrate 55 g Dietary Fiber 12 g Protein 6 g Total Sugars 29 g Potassium 1051 mg

Coconut & Strawberry Smoothie

Preparation Time: 10 Minutes
Cooking Time: 0 minutes
Serves: 1
Calories: 278
Protein: 14 Grams
Fat: 2 Grams
Carbs: 57 Grams
Ingredients:
1 Cup Strawberries, Frozen & Thawed Slightly
1 Ripe Banana, Sliced & Frozen
½ Cup Coconut Milk, Light
½ Cup Vegan Yogurt

1 Tablespoon Chia Seeds
1 Teaspoon Lime juice, Fresh
4 Ice Cubes
Directions:
Blend everything together until smooth, and serve immediately.

Pumpkin Chia Smoothie

Preparation Time: 5 Minutes
Cooking Time: 0 minutes
Serves: 1
Calories: 726
Protein: 5.5 Grams
Fat: 69.8 Grams
Carbs: 15 Grams
Ingredients:
3 Tablespoons Pumpkin Puree
1 Tablespoon MCT Oil
¾ Cup Coconut Milk, Full Fat
½ Avocado, Fresh
1 Teaspoon Vanilla, Pure
½ Teaspoon Pumpkin Pie Spice
Directions:
Combine all ingredients together until blended.

Cantaloupe Smoothie Bowl

Preparation Time: 5 Minutes
Cooking Time: 0 minutes
Serves: 2
Calories: 135
Protein: 3 Grams
Fat: 1 Gram
Carbs: 32 Grams
Ingredients:
¾ Cup carrot Juice
4 Cps Cantaloupe, Frozen & Cubed
Mellon Balls or Berries to Serve
Pinch Sea Salt
Directions:
Blend everything together until smooth.

Berry & Cauliflower Smoothie

Preparation Time: 10 Minutes
Cooking Time: 0 minutes
Serves: 2
Calories: 149
Protein: 3 Grams
Fat: 3 Grams
Carbs: 29 Grams
Ingredients:
1 Cup Riced Cauliflower, Frozen
1 Cup Banana, Sliced & Frozen
½ Cup Mixed Berries, Frozen
2 Cups Almond Milk, Unsweetened
2 Teaspoons Maple syrup, Pure & Optional
Directions:
Blend until mixed well.

Green Mango Smoothie

Preparation Time: 5 Minutes
Cooking Time: 0 minutes
Serves: 1
Calories: 417
Protein: 7.2 Grams
Fat: 2.8 Grams
Carbs: 102.8 Grams
Ingredients:
2 Cups Spinach
1-2 Cups Coconut Water
2 Mangos, Ripe, Peeled & Diced
Directions:
Blend everything together until smooth.

Chia Seed Smoothie

Preparation Time: 5 Minutes
Cooking Time: 0 minutes
Serves: 3
Calories: 477
Protein: 8 Grams
Fat: 29 Grams
Carbs: 57 Grams
Ingredients:
¼ Teaspoon Cinnamon
1 Tablespoon Ginger, Fresh & Grated
Pinch Cardamom
1 Tablespoon Chia Seeds
2 Medjool Dates, Pitted
1 Cup Alfalfa Sprouts
1 Cup Water
1 Banana
½ Cup Coconut Milk, Unsweetened
Directions:
Blend everything together until smooth.

Mango Smoothie

Preparation Time: 5 Minutes
Cooking Time: 0 minutes
Serves: 3
Calories: 376
Protein: 5 Grams
Fat: 2 Grams
Carbs: 95 Grams
Ingredients:
1 Carrot, Peeled & Chopped
1 Cup Strawberries
1 Cup Water
1 Cup Peaches, Chopped
1 Banana, Frozen & sliced
1 Cup Mango, Chopped
Directions:
Blend everything together until smooth.

Chocolate Smoothie

Preparation Time: 5 min.
Cooking Time: 5 min.
Servings: 2
Ingredients:

¼ c. almond butter
¼ c. cocoa powder, unsweetened
½ c. coconut milk, canned
1 c. almond milk, unsweetened
Directions:
Before making the smoothie, freeze the almond milk into cubes using an ice cube tray. This would take a few hours, so prepare it ahead.
Blend everything using your preferred machine until it reaches your desired thickness.
Serve immediately and enjoy!
Nutrition: Calories: 147 | Carbohydrates: 8.2 g | Proteins: 4 g | Fats: 13.4 g

Chocolate Mint Smoothie

Preparation Time: 5 min.
Cooking Time: 5 min.
Serving: 1
Ingredients:
2 tbsp. sweetener of your choice
2 drops mint extract
1 tbsp. cocoa powder
½ avocado, medium
¼ c. coconut milk
1 c. almond milk, unsweetened
Directions:
In a high-speed blender, add all the ingredients and blend until smooth.
Add two to four ice cubes and blend.
Serve immediately and enjoy!
Nutrition: Calories: 401 | Carbohydrates: 6.3 g | Proteins: 5 g | Fats: 40.3 g

Cinnamon Roll Smoothie

Preparation Time: 2 min.
Cooking Time: 2 min.
Serving: 1
Ingredients:
1 t. cinnamon
1 scoop vanilla protein powder
½ c. of the following:
almond milk, unsweetened
coconut milk
Sweetener of your choice

Directions:
In a high-speed blender, add all the ingredients and blend.
Add two to four ice cubes and blend until smooth.
Serve immediately and enjoy!
Nutrition: Calories: 507 | Carbohydrates: 17 g | Proteins: 33.3 g | Fats: 34.9 g

Coconut Smoothie

Preparation Time: 2 min.
Cooking Time: 2 min.
Servings: 2
Ingredients:
1 t. chia seeds
1/8 c. almonds, soaked
1 c. coconut milk
1 avocado
Directions:
In a high-speed blender, add all the ingredients and blend until smooth.
Add your desired number of ice cubes, depending on your favored consistency, of course, and blend again.
Serve immediately and enjoy!
Nutrition: Calories: 584 | Carbohydrates: 22.5 g | Proteins: 8.3 g | Fats: 55.5g

Maca Almond Smoothie

Preparation Time: 5 min.
Cooking Time: 5 min.
Servings: 2
Ingredients:
½ t. vanilla extract
1 scoop maca powder
1 tbsp. almond butter
1 c. almond milk, unsweetened
2 avocados
Directions:
In a high-speed blender, add all the ingredients and blend until smooth.

Serve immediately and enjoy!
Nutrition: Calories: 758 | Carbohydrates: 28 g | Proteins: 9.3 g | Fats: 72.3 g

Blueberry Smoothie

Preparation Time: 5 min.
Cooking Time: 5 min.
Serving: 1
Ingredients:
¼ c. pumpkin seeds shelled unsalted
3 c. blueberries, frozen
2 avocados, peeled and halved
1 c. almond milk
Directions:
In a high-speed blender, add all the ingredients and blend until smooth.
Add two to four ice cubes and blend until smooth.
Serve immediately and enjoy!
Nutrition: Calories: 401 | Carbohydrates: 6.3 g | Proteins: 5 g | Fats: 40.3 g

Nutty Protein Shake

Preparation Time: 5 min.
Cooking Time: 5 min.
Serving: 1
Ingredients:
¼ avocado
2 tbsp. powdered peanut butter
1 tbsp. of the following:
Cocoa powder
Peanut butter
1 scoop protein powder
½ c. almond milk
Directions:

In a high-speed blender, add all the ingredients and blend until smooth.
Add two to four ice cubes and blend again.
Serve immediately and enjoy!
Nutrition: Calories: 694 | Carbohydrates: 30 g | Proteins: 40.8 g | Fats: 52 g

Cinnamon Pear Smoothie

Preparation Time: 2 min.
Cooking Time: 2 min.
Serving: 1
Ingredients:
1 t. cinnamon
1 scoop vanilla protein powder
½ c. of the following:
Almond milk, unsweetened
Coconut Milk
2 pears, cores removed
Sweetener of your choice
Directions:
In a high-speed blender, add all the ingredients and blend.
Add two or more ice cubes and blend again.
Serve immediately and enjoy!
Nutrition: Calories: 653 | Carbohydrates: 75.2 g | Proteins: 28.4 g | Fats: 32.2 g

Vanilla Milkshake

Preparation Time: 5 min.
Cooking Time: 5 min.
Servings: 4
Ingredients:
2 c. ice cubes
2 t. vanilla extract
6 tbsp. powdered erythritol
1 c. cream of dairy-free
½ c. coconut milk
Directions:
In a high-speed blender, add all the ingredients and blend.
Add ice cubes and blend until smooth.
Serve immediately and enjoy!
Nutrition: Calories: 125 | Carbohydrates: 6.8 g | Proteins: 1.2 g | Fats: 11.5 g

Raspberry Protein Shake

Preparation Time: 5 min.
Cooking Time: 5 min.
Serving: 1
Ingredients:
¼ avocado
1 c. raspberries, frozen

1 scoop protein powder

½ c. almond milk

Ice cubes

Directions:

In a high-speed blender add all the ingredients and blend until lumps of fruit disappear.

Add two to four ice cubes and blend to your desired consistency.

Serve immediately and enjoy!

Nutrition: Calories: 756 | Carbohydrates: 80.1 g | Proteins: 27.6 g | Fats: 40.7 g

Raspberry Almond Smoothie

Preparation Time: 5 min.

Cooking Time: 5 min.

Serving: 1

Ingredients:

10 Almonds, finely chopped

3 tbsp. almond butter

1 c. almond milk

1 c. Raspberries, frozen

Directions:

In a high-speed blender, add all the ingredients and blend until smooth.

Serve immediately and enjoy!

Nutrition: Calories: 449 | Carbohydrates: 26 g | Proteins: 14 g | Fats: 35 g

Dinner Recipes

Mushroom Steak

Preparation Time: 30 min.
Cooking Time: 1 hr.
Servings: 8
Ingredients:
1 tbsp. of the following:
fresh lemon juice
olive oil, extra virgin
2 tbsp. coconut oil
3 thyme sprigs
8 medium Portobello mushrooms
For Sauce:
1 ½ t. of the following:
minced garlic
minced peeled fresh ginger
2 tbsp. of the following:
light brown sugar
mirin
½ c. low-sodium soy sauce

Directions:
For the sauce, combine all the sauce ingredients, along with ¼ cup water into a little pan and simmer to cook. Cook using a medium heat until it reduces to a glaze, approximately 15 to 20 minutes, then remove from the heat.

For the mushrooms, bring the oven to 350 heat setting.

Using a skillet, melt coconut oil and olive oil, cooking the mushrooms on each side for about 3 minutes.

Next, arrange the mushrooms in a single layer on a sheet for baking and season with lemon juice, salt, and pepper.

Carefully slide into the oven and roast for 5 minutes. Let it rest for 2 minutes.

Plate and drizzle the sauce over the mushrooms.

Enjoy.

Nutrition: Calories: 87 | Carbohydrates: 6.2 g | Proteins: 3 g | Fats: 6.2 g

Spicy Grilled Tofu Steak

Preparation Time: 30 min.
Cooking Time: 20 min.
Servings: 4
Ingredients:
1 tbsp. of the following:
chopped scallion
chopped cilantro
soy sauce
hoisin sauce
2 tbsp. oil
¼ t. of the following:
salt
garlic powder
red chili pepper powder
ground Sichuan peppercorn powder
½ t. cumin
1 pound firm tofu
Directions:
Place the tofu on a plate and drain the excess liquid for about 10 minutes.

Slice drained tofu into ¾ thick stakes.

Stir the cumin, Sichuan peppercorn, chili powder, garlic powder, and salt in a mixing bowl until well-incorporated.

In another little bowl, combine soy sauce, hoisin, and 1 teaspoon of oil.

Heat a skillet to medium temperature with oil, then carefully place the tofu in the skillet.

Sprinkle the spices over the tofu, distributing equally across all steaks. Cook for 3-5 minutes, flip, and put spice on the other side. Cook for an additional 3 minutes.

Brush with sauce and plate.

Sprinkle some scallion and cilantro and enjoy.

Nutrition: Calories: 155 | Carbohydrates: 7.6 g | Proteins: 9.9 g | Fats: 11.8g

Piquillo Salsa Verde Steak

Preparation Time: 30 min.
Cooking Time: 25 min.
Yields: 8 Servings
Ingredients:
4 – ½ inch thick slices of ciabatta
18 oz. firm tofu, drained
5 tbsp. olive oil, extra virgin
Pinch of cayenne
½ t. cumin, ground
1 ½ tbsp. sherry vinegar
1 shallot, diced
8 piquillo peppers (can be from a jar) – drained and cut to ½ inch strips
3 tbsp. of the following:
parsley, finely chopped
capers, drained and chopped

Directions:
Place the tofu on a plate to drain the excess liquid, and then slice into 8 rectangle pieces.

You can either prepare your grill or use a grill pan. If using a grill pan, preheat the grill pan.

Mix 3 tablespoons of olive oil, cayenne, cumin, vinegar, shallot, parsley, capers, and piquillo peppers in a medium bowl to make our salsa verde. Season to preference with salt and pepper.

Using a paper towel, dry the tofu slices.

Brush olive oil on each side, seasoning with salt and pepper lightly.

Place the bread on the grill and toast for about 2 minutes using medium-high heat.

Next, grill the tofu, cooking each side for about 3 minutes or until the tofu is heated through.

Place the toasted bread on the plate then the tofu on top of the bread.

Gently spoon out the salsa verde over the tofu and serve.

Nutrition: Calories: 427 | Carbohydrates: 67.5 g | Proteins: 14.2 g | Fats: 14.6 g

Butternut Squash Steak

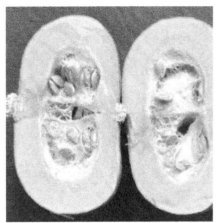

Preparation Time: 30 min.
Cooking Time: 50 min.
Servings: 4
Ingredients:
2 tbsp. coconut yogurt
½ t. sweet paprika
1 ¼ c. low-sodium vegetable broth
1 sprig thyme
1 finely chopped garlic clove
1 big thinly sliced shallot
1 tbsp. margarine
2 tbsp. olive oil, extra virgin
Salt and pepper to liking
irections:
Bring the oven to 375 heat setting.

Cut the squash, lengthwise, into 4 steaks.

Carefully core one side of each squash with a paring knife in a crosshatch pattern.

Using a brush, coat with olive oil each side of the steak then season generously with salt and pepper.

In an oven-safe, non-stick skillet, bring 2 tablespoons of olive oil to a warm temperature.

Place the steaks on the skillet with the cored side down and cook at medium temperature until browned, approximately 5 minutes.

Flip and repeat on the other side for about 3 minutes.

Place the skillet into the oven to roast the squash for 7 minutes.

Take out from the oven, placing on a plate and covering with aluminum foil to keep warm.

Using the previously used skillet, add thyme, garlic, and shallot, cooking at medium heat. Stir frequently for about 2 minutes.

Add brandy and cook for an additional minute.

Next, add paprika and whisk the mixture together for 3 minutes.

Add in the yogurt seasoning with salt and pepper.

Plate the steaks and spoon the sauce over the top.

Garnish with parsley and enjoy!

Nutrition: Calories: 300 | Carbohydrates: 46 g | Proteins: 5.3 g | Fats: 10.6g

Cauliflower Steak Kicking Corn

Preparation Time: 30 min.
Cooking Time: 60 min.
Servings: 6
Ingredients:
2 t. capers, drained
4 scallions, chopped
1 red chili, minced
¼ c. vegetable oil
2 ears of corn, shucked
2 big cauliflower heads
Salt and pepper to taste

Directions:
Heat the oven to 375 degrees.

Boil a pot of water, about 4 cups, using the maximum heat setting available.

Add corn in the saucepan, cooking approximately 3 minutes or until tender.

Drain and allow the corn to cool, then slice the kernels away from the cob.

Warm 2 tablespoons of vegetable oil in a skillet.

Combine the chili pepper with the oil, cooking for approximately 30 seconds.

Next, combine the scallions, sautéing with the chili pepper until soft.

Mix in the corn and capers in the skillet and cook for approximately 1 minute to blend the flavors. Then remove from heat.

Warm 1 tablespoon of vegetable oil in a skillet. Once warm, begin to place cauliflower steaks to the pan, 2 to 3 at a time. Season to your liking with salt and cook over medium heat for 3 minutes or until lightly browned.

Once cooked, slide onto the cookie sheet and repeat step 5 with the remaining cauliflower.

Take the corn mixture and press into the spaces between the florets of the cauliflower.

Bake for 25 minutes.

Serve warm and enjoy!

Nutrition: Calories: 153 | Carbohydrates: 15 g | Proteins: 4 g | Fats: 10 g

Pistachio Watermelon Steak

Preparation Time: 5 min.
Cooking Time: 10 min.
Servings: 4
Ingredients:
Microgreens
Pistachios chopped
Malden sea salt
1 tbsp. olive oil, extra virgin
1 watermelon
Salt to taste

Directions:
Begin by cutting the ends of the watermelon.

Carefully peel the skin from the watermelon along the white outer edge.

Slice the watermelon into 4 slices, approximately 2 inches thick.

Trim the slices, so they are rectangular in shape approximately 2 x4 inches.

Heat a skillet to medium heat add 1 tablespoon of olive oil.

Add watermelon steaks and cook until the edges begin to caramelize.

Plate and top with pistachios and microgreens.

Sprinkle with Malden salt.
Serve warm and enjoy!
Nutrition: Calories: 67 | Carbohydrates: 3.8 g | Proteins: 1.6 g Fats: 5.9 g

Bbq Ribs

Preparation Time: 30 min.
Cooking Time: 45 min.
Servings: 2
Ingredients:
2 drops liquid smoke
2 tbsp. of the following:
soy sauce
tahini
1 c. of the following:
water
wheat gluten
1 tbsp. of the following:
garlic powder
onion powder
lemon pepper
2 t. chipotle powder
For the Sauce:
2 chipotle peppers in adobo, minced
1 tbsp. of the following:
vegan Worcestershire sauce
lemon juice
horseradish
onion powder
garlic powder
ground pepper
1 t. dry mustard
2 tbsp. sweetener of your choice
5 tbsp. brown sugar
½ c. apple cider vinegar
2 c. ketchup
1 c. water
1 freshly squeezed orange juice
Directions:
Set the oven to 350 heat setting, and prepare the grill charcoal as recommended for this, but gas will work as well.

Combine soy sauce, tahini, water, and liquid smoke in a bowl. Then set this mixture to the side in a mixing bowl.

Next, use a big glass bowl to mix chipotle powder, onion powder, lemon pepper, garlic powder; combine well then whisk in the ingredients from the little bowl.

Add the wheat gluten and mix until it comes to a gooey consistency.

Grease a standard-size loaf pan and transfer the mixture to the loaf pan. Smooth it out so that the rib mixture fits flat in the pan.

Bake for 30 minutes.

While the mixture is baking, make the BBQ sauce. To make the sauce, combine all the sauce ingredients in a pot. Allow the mixture to simmer its way to the boiling point to combine the flavors, and as soon as it boils, decrease the heat to the minimum setting. Let it be for 10 more minutes.

Cautiously take the rib out of the oven and slide onto a plate.

Coat the top rib mixture with the BBQ Sauce and place on the grill.

Coat the other side of the rib mixture with BBQ Sauce and grill for 6 minutes

Flip and grill the other side for an additional 6 minutes.

Serve warm and enjoy!
Nutrition: Calories: 649 | Carbohydrates: 114 g | Proteins: 34.8 g | Fats: 11.1g

Spicy Veggie Steaks With Veggies

Preparation Time: 30 min.
Cooking Time: 45 mins.
Servings: 4
Ingredients:
1 ¾ c. vital wheat gluten
½ c. vegetable stock
¼ t. liquid smoke
1 tbsp. Dijon mustard
1 t. paprika
½ c. tomato paste
2 tbsp. soy sauce
½ t. oregano
¼ t. of the following:
coriander powder
cumin
1 t. of the following:
onion powder
garlic powder
¼ c. nutritional yeast
¾ c. canned chickpeas
Marinade:
½ t. red pepper flakes
2 cloves garlic, minced
2 tbsp. soy sauce
1 tbsp. lemon juice, freshly squeezed
¼ c. maple syrup
For skewers:
15 skewers, soaked in water for 30 minutes if wooden
¾ t. salt

8 oz. zucchini or yellow summer squash
¼ t. ground black pepper
1 tbsp. olive oil
1 red onion, medium

Directions:

In a food processor, add chickpeas, vegetable stock, liquid smoke, Dijon mustard, pepper, paprika, tomato paste, soy sauce, oregano, coriander, cumin, onion powder, garlic, and natural yeast. Process until the ingredients are well-mixed.

Add the vital wheat gluten to a big mixing bowl, and pour the contents from the food processor into the center. Mix with a spoon until a soft dough is formed.

Knead the dough for approximately 2 minutes; do not over knead.

Once the dough is firm and stretchy, flatten it to create 4 equal-sized steaks.

Individually wrap the steaks in tin foil; be sure not to wrap the steaks too tightly, as they will expand when steaming.

Steam for 20 minutes. To steam, you can use any steamer you like or a basket over boiling water.

While steaming, prepare the marinade. In a bowl, whisk the red pepper, garlic, soy sauce, lemon juice, and syrup. Reserve half of the sauce for brushing during grilling.

Prepare the skewers. Cut the onion and zucchini or yellow squash into 1/2-inch chunks.

In a glass bowl, add the red onion, zucchini, and yellow squash then coat with olive oil, pepper, and salt to taste. Place the vegetables on the skewers.

After the steaks have steamed for 20 minutes, unwrap and place on a cookie sheet. Pour the marinade over the steaks, fully covering them.

Bring your skewers, steaks, and glaze to the grill. Place the skewers on the grill over direct heat. Brush skewers with glaze. Grill for approximately 3 minutes then flip.

Place the steaks directly on the grill, glaze side down, and brush the top with additional glaze. Cook to your desired doneness.

Serve warm and enjoy!

Nutrition: Calories: 458 | Carbohydrates: 65.5 g | Proteins: 39.1 g | Fats: 7.6 g

Broccoli & black beans stir fry

Preparation time 60 minutes
Cooking time: 10 minutes
Servings: 6
Ingredients:
4 cups broccoli flore ts
2 cups cooked black beans
1 tablespoon sesame oil
4 teaspoons sesame seeds
2 cloves garlic, finely minced
2 teaspoons ginger, finely chopped
A large pinch red chili flakes
A pinch turmeric powder
Salt to taste
Lime juice to taste (optional)
Direction:

Steam broccoli for 6 minutes. Drain and set aside.

Warm the sesame oil in a large frying pan over medium heat. Add sesame seeds, chili flakes, ginger, garlic, turmeric powder, and salt. Sauté for a couple of minutes.

Add broccoli and black beans and sauté until thoroughly heated.

Sprinkle lime juice and serve hot.

Stuffed peppers

Preparation time 40 minutes
Cooking time: 15 minutes
Servings: 8
Ingredients:
2 cans (15 ounces each) black beans, drained, rinsed
2 cups tofu, pressed, crumbled
3/4 cup green onion s, thinly sliced
1/2 cup fresh cilantro, chopped
1/4 cup vegetable oil
1/4 cup lime juice
3 cloves garlic, finely chopped
1/2 teaspoon salt
1/2 teaspoon chili powder
8 large bell peppers, halved lengthwise, deseeded
3 roma tomatoes, diced
Direction:

Mix together in a bowl all the ingredients except the bell peppers to make the filling.

Fill the peppers with this mixture.

Cut 8 aluminum foils of size 18 x 12 inches. Place 2 halves on each aluminum foil. Seal the peppers such that there is a gap on the sides.

Grill under direct heat for about 15 minutes.

Sprinkle with some cilantro and serve.

Sweet 'n spicy tofu

Preparation time 45 minutes
Cooking time: 10 minutes
Servings: 8
Ingredients:
14 ounces extra firm tofu; press the excess liquid and chop into cubes.
3 tablespoons olive oil
2 2-3 cloves garlic, minced
4 tablespoons sriracha sauce or any other hot sauce
2 tablespoons soy sauce
1/4 cup sweet chili sauce
5-6 cups mixed vegetables of your choice (like carrots, cauliflower, broccoli, potato, etc.)
Salt to taste (optional)

Direction:
Place a nonstick pan over medium-high heat. Add 1 tablespoon oil. When oil is hot, add garlic and mixed vegetables and stir-fry until crisp and tender. Remove and keep aside.

Place the pan back on heat. Add 2 tablespoons oil. When oil is hot, add tofu and sauté until golden brown. Add the sautéed vegetables. Mix well and remove from heat.

Make a mixture of sauces by mixing together all the sauces in a small bowl.

Serve the stir fried vegetables and tofu with sauce.

Eggplant & mushrooms in peanut sauce

Preparation time 32 minutes
Cooking time: 10 minutes
Servings: 6

Ingredients:
4 Japanese eggplants cut into 1-inch thick round slices
3/4 pounds of shiitake mu shrooms, stems discarded, halved
3 tablespoons smooth peanut butter
2 1/2 tablespoons rice vinegar
1 1/2 tablespoons soy sauce
1 1/2 tablespoons, peeled, fresh ginger, finely grated
1 1/2 tablespoons light brown sugar
Coarse salt to taste
3 scallions, cut into 2-inch lengths, thinly sliced lengthwise
Direction:
Place the eggplants and mushroom in a steamer. Steam the eggplant and mushrooms until tender. Transfer to a bowl.

To a small bowl, add peanut butter and vinegar and whisk.

Add rest of the ingredients and whisk well. Add this to the bowl of eggplant slices. Add scallions and mix well.

Serve hot.

Green beans stir fry

Preparation time 30 minutes
Cooking time: 10 minutes
Servings: 6-8
Ingredients:
1 1/2 pounds of green beans, stringed, chopped into 1 ½-inch pieces
1 large onion, thinly sliced
4 star anise (optional)
3 tablespoons avocado oil
1 1/2 tablespoons tamari sauce or soy sauce
Salt to taste
3/4 cup water
Direction:
Place a wok over medium heat. Add oil. When oil is heated, add onions and sauté until onions are translucent.

Add beans, water, tamari sauce, and star anise and stir. Cover and cook until the beans are tender.

Uncover, add salt and raise the heat to high. Cook until the water dries up in the wok. Stir a couple of times while cooking.

Collard greens 'n tofu

Preparation time 15 minutes
Cooking time: 20 minutes

Servings: 4
Ingredients:
2 pounds of collard greens, rinsed, chopped
1 cup water
1/2 pound of tofu, chopped
Salt to taste
Pepper powder to taste
Crushed red chili to taste
Direction:
Place a large skillet over medium-high heat. Add oil. When the oil is heated, add tofu and cook until brown.

Add rest of the ingredients and mix well.
Cook until greens wilts and almost dry.

Cassoulet

Preparation time: 35 minutes
Cooking time: 1 hr and 30 minutes
Servings: 4
Protein content per serving: 22 g
Ingredients
¼ cup (60 ml) olive oil, divided
4 ounces (113 g) quit-the-cluck seitan, chopped
1/3 of a smoky sausage, chopped
1½ cups (240 g) chopped onion
2 ounces (57 g) minced shiitake mushrooms
2 large carrots, peeled, sliced into ¼-inch (6 mm) rounds
2 stalks celery, chopped
1½ cups (355 ml) vegetable broth, divided
1 teaspoon liquid smoke
3 cans (each 15 ounces, or 425 g) white beans of choice, drained and rinsed
1 can (14.5 ounces, or 410 g) diced tomatoes, undrained
2 tablespoons (32 g) tomato paste 1 tablespoon (15 ml) tamari
1 tablespoon (18 g) no chicken bouillon paste, or 2 bouillon cubes, crumbled
2 tablespoons (8 g) minced fresh parsley
2 teaspoons dried thyme
½ teaspoon dried rosemary salt and pepper
2 cups (200 g) fresh bread crumbs
½ cup (40 g) panko crumbs
Direction
Preheat the oven to 375°f (190°c, or gas mark 5).

Heat 1 tablespoon (15 ml) of olive oil in a large skillet over medium heat.

Add the seitan and sausage. Cook for 4 to 6 minutes, occasionally stirring, until browned. Transfer to a plate and set aside.

Add the onion and a pinch of salt to the same skillet. Cook for 5 to 7 minutes until translucent. Transfer to the same plate. Add the shiitakes, carrots, and celery to the skillet and cook for 2 minutes. Add 1 tablespoon (15 ml) vegetable broth and the liquid smoke. Cook for 2 to 3 minutes, stirring until the liquid is absorbed or evaporated.

Return the seitan and onions to the skillet and add the beans, tomatoes, tomato paste, tamari, bouillon, parsley, thyme, rosemary, and remaining broth. Cook for 3 to 4 minutes, stirring to combine. Season with salt and pepper to taste and transfer to a large casserole pan.

Toss together the fresh bread crumbs, panko crumbs, and the remaining 3 tablespoons (45 ml) olive oil in a small bowl. Spread evenly over the bean mixture. Bake for 30 to 35 minutes until the crumbs are browned.

Double-garlic bean and vegetable soup

Preparation time: 25 minutes
Cooking time: 10 minutes
Servings: 4
Protein content per serving: 21 g
Ingredients
1 tablespoon (15 ml) olive oil
1 teaspoon fine sea salt
1 (240 g) minced onion 5 cloves garlic, minced
2 cups (220 g) chopped red potatoes
⅔ cup (96 g) sliced carrots
Protein content per serving cup (60 g) chopped celery
1 teaspoon italian seasoning blend
Protein content per serving teaspoon red pepper flakes, or to taste
Protein content per serving teaspoon celery seed
4 cups water (940 ml), divided
1 can (14.5 ounces, or 410 g) crushed tomatoes or tomato puree
1 head roasted garlic
2 tablespoons (30 g) prepared vegan pesto, plus more for garnish
2 cans (each 15 ounces, or 425 g) different kinds of white beans, drained and rinsed
Protein content per serving cup (50 g)
1-inch (2.5 cm) pieces green beans
Salt and pepper
Directions:
Heat the oil and salt in a large soup pot over medium heat. Add the onion, garlic, potatoes, carrots, and celery. Cook for 4 to 6 minutes,

occasionally stirring, until the onions are translucent. Add the seasoning blend, red pepper flakes, and celery seed and stir for 2 minutes. Add 3 cups (705 ml) of the water and the crushed tomatoes.

Combine the remaining 1 cup (235 ml) water and the roasted garlic in a blender. Process until smooth. Add to the soup mixture and bring to a boil. Reduce the heat to simmer and cook for 30 minutes.

Stir in the pesto, beans, and green beans. Simmer for 15 minutes. Taste and adjust the seasonings. Serve each bowl with a dollop of pesto, if desired.

Mean bean minestrone

Preparation time: 45 minutes
Cooking time: 40 minutes
Servings: 6
Protein content per serving: 9g
Ingredients
1 tablespoon (15 ml) olive oil
1/3 cup (80 g) chopped red onion
4 cloves garlic, grated or pressed
1 leek, white and light green parts, trimmed and chopped (about 4 ounces, or 113 g)
2 carrots, peeled and minced (about 4 ounces, or 113 g)
2 ribs of celery, minced (about 2 ounces, or 57 g)
2 yellow squashes, trimmed and chopped (about 8 ounces, or 227 g)
1 green bell pepper, trimmed and chopped (about 8 ounces, or 227 g)
1 tablespoon (16 g) tomato paste
1 teaspoon dried oregano
1 teaspoon dried basil
⅓ teaspoon smoked paprika
¼ To ¼ teaspoon cayenne pepper, or to taste
2 cans (each 15 ounces, or 425 g) diced fire-roasted tomatoes
4 cups (940 ml) vegetable broth, more if needed
3 cups (532 g) cannellini beans, or other white beans
2 cups (330 g) cooked farro, or other whole grain or pasta
Salt, to taste
Nut and seed sprinkles, for garnish, optional and to taste
Directions:
In a large pot, add the oil, onion, garlic, leek, carrots, celery, yellow squash, bell pepper, tomato paste, oregano, basil, paprika, and cayenne pepper. Cook on medium-high heat, stirring often until the vegetables start to get tender, about 6 minutes.

Add the tomatoes and broth. Bring to a boil, lower the heat, cover with a lid, and simmer 15 minutes.

Add the beans and simmer another 10 minutes. Add the farro and simmer 5 more minutes to heat the farro.

Note that this is a thick minestrone. If there are leftovers (which taste even better, by the way), the soup will thicken more once chilled.

Add extra broth if you prefer a thinner soup and adjust seasoning if needed. Add nut and seed sprinkles on each portion upon serving, if desired.

Store leftovers in an airtight container in the refrigerator for up to 5 days. The minestrone can also be frozen for up to 3 months.

Snacks and Desserts

Mango And Banana Shake

Preparation time: 10 mins
Cooking time: 0 mins
Servings: 2
Ingredients:
1 Banana, Sliced And Frozen
1 Cup Frozen Mango Chunks
1 Cup Almond Milk
1 Tbsp. Maple Syrup
1 Tsp Lime Juice
2-4 Raspberries For Topping
Mango Slice For Topping
Directions
In blender, pulse banana, mango with milk, maple syrup, lime juice until smooth but still thick
Add more liquid if needed.
Pour shake into 2 bowls.
Top with berries and mango slice.
Enjoy!
Nutrition: Protein: 5% 8 kcal Fat: 11% 18 kcal Carbohydrates: 85% 140 kcal

Avocado Toast With Flaxseeds

Preparation time: 5 mins.
Cooking time: 0 mins
Servings: 3
Ingredients:
3 slice of whole grain bread
1 large avocado, ripe
¼ cup chopped parsley
1 tbsp. flax seeds
1 tbsp. sesame seeds
1 tbsp. lime juice
Directions:
First, toast your piece of bread.
Remove the avocado seed.
Slice half avocado and mash half avocado with fork in bowl.
Spread mashed avocado on 2 toasted bread.
Place avocado slice on 1 toast.
Top with flax seeds and sesame seeds.
Drizzle lime juice and chopped parsley on top.
Serve and enjoy!
Nutrition: Protein: 12% 31 kcal Fat: 49% 124 kcal Carbohydrates: 39% 98 kcal

Avocado Hummus

Preparation time: 10 mins
Cooking time:
Servings: 4
Ingredients
2 Ripe Avocados
½ Cup Coconut Cream
¼ Cup Sesame Paste
½ Lemon Juice
1 Tsp. Clove, Pressed
½ Tsp Ground Cumin
½ Tsp Salt
¼ Tsp Ground Black Pepper
Directions
Cut the avocado lengthways and remove seed from the fruit.
Put all ingredients in a blender or food processor and mix until thoroughly smooth.
Add more cream, lemon juice or water if you want to have a looser texture.
Adjust seasonings as needed.
Serve with naan and enjoy.
Nutrition: Protein: 6% 21 kcal Fat: 79% 289 kcal Carbohydrates: 16% 57 kcal

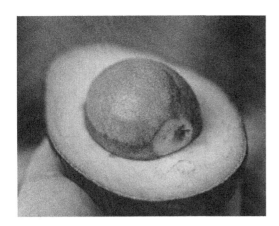

Plant Based Crispy Falafel

Preparation time: 20 mins
Cooking time: 30 mins
Servings: 8
Ingredients
1 tbsp. extra-virgin olive oil
1 cup dried chickpeas soaked for 24 hours in the refrigerator
1 cup cauliflower, chopped
½ cup red onion, chopped
½ cup packed fresh parsley
2 cloves garlic, quartered
1 tsp. sea salt
½ tsp. ground black pepper
½ tsp. ground cumin
¼ tsp. ground cinnamon
Directions
Preheat oven to 375° F.
In a food processor, mix chickpeas, cauliflower, onion, parsley, garlic, salt, pepper, cumin seeds, cinnamon, and olive oil until mixture is smooth.
Take 2 tbsps. of mixture and make the falafel into small patties.
Keep falafel on greased baking tray.
Bake falafel for about 25 to 30 minutes in preheated oven until golden brown from both sides.
Once cooked remove from oven.
Serve hot fresh vegetable salad and enjoy!
Nutrition: Protein: 16% 19 kcal Fat: 24% 29 kcal Carbohydrates: 60% 71 kcal

Waffles With Almond Flour

Preparation time: 15 mins
Cooking time: 15 mins
Servings: 4
Ingredients
1 cup almond milk

2 tbsps. chia seeds
2 tsp lemon juice
4 tbsps. coconut oil
1/2 cup almond flour
2 tbsps. maple syrup
Cooking spray or cooking oil

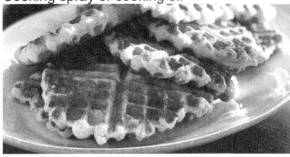

Directions
Mix coconut milk with lemon juice in a mixing bowl.
Leave it for 5-8 minutes on room temperature to turn it into butter milk.
Once coconut milk is turned into butter milk, add chai seeds into milk and whisk together.
Add other ingredients in milk mixture and mix well.
Preheat a waffle iron and spray it with coconut oil spray.
Pour 2 tbsp. of waffle mixture into the waffle machine and cook until golden.
Top with some berries and serve hot.
Enjoy with black coffee!
Nutrition: Protein: 5% 15 kcal Fat: 71% 199 kcal Carbohydrates: 23% 66 kcal

Mint & Avocado Smoothie

Preparation time: 10 mins
Cooking time: 0 minutes

Servings: 2
Ingredients
1 cup coconut water
1/2 lemon juice
½ cup cucumber
1 cup mint. fresh
1/2 medium size avocado
l/2 tsp maple syrup
1 cup ice
Directions
Place all ingredients into a blender, cover lid and blend until smooth.

Blend on high speed until smoothie has fluffy texture.

Pour smoothie in glass and top with mint leaves.

Serve and enjoy!

Nutrition: Protein: 6% 7 kcal Fat: 51% 64 kcal Carbohydrates: 44% 55 kcal

Simple Banana Fritters

Preparation time: 15 mins
Cooking time: 20 mins
Servings: 8
Ingredients
4 Bananas
3 Tbsps. Maple Syrup
¼ Tsp. Cinnamon Powder
¼ Tsp. Nutmeg
1 Cup Coconut Flour

Directions
Preheat oven to 350° F.

Mash the bananas in a large mixing bowl along with maple syrup, cinnamon, nutmeg powder and coconut flour.

Mix all the ingredients well.

Take 2 tbsps. mixture and make small 1-inch-thick fritters from this mixture.

Place fritters in greased baking tray.

Bake fritters in preheated oven for about 10-15 minutes until golden from both sides.

Once done, take them out of the oven.
Serve with coconut cream.
Enjoy!
Nutrition: Protein: 3% 3 kcal Fat: 28% 30 kcal Carbohydrates: 69% 75 kcal

Coconut And Blueberries Ice Cream

Preparation time: 5 mins
Cooking time: 0 mins
Servings: 4
Ingredients
1/4 Cup Coconut Cream
1 Tbsp. Maple Syrup
¼ Cup Coconut Flour
1 Cup Blueberries
¼ Cup Blueberries For Topping
Directions
Put ingredients into food processor and mix well on high speed.

Pour mixture in silicon molds and freeze in freezer for about 2-4 hours.

Once balls are set remove from freezer.

Top with berries.

Serve cold and enjoy!

Nutrition: Protein: 3% 4 kcal Fat: 40% 60 kcal Carbohydrates: 57% 86 kcal

Peach Crockpot Pudding

Preparation time: 15 mins
Cooking time: 4 hours
Servings: 6
Ingredients
2 Cups Sliced Peaches
1/4 Cup Maple Syrup
/2 Tsp. Cinnamon Powder
2 Cups Coconut Milk
For Serving
½ Cup Coconut Cream
1 Oz. Coconut Flakes

Directions
Lightly grease the crockpot and place peaches in the bottom.

Add maple syrup, cinnamon powder and milk.

Cover and cook on high for 4 hours.

Once cooked remove from crockpot.

For serving pour coconut cream.

Top with coconut flakes.

Serve and enjoy!

Nutrition: Protein: 3% 11 kcal Fat: 61% 230 kcal Carbohydrates: 36% 133 kcal

Healthy Chocolate Mousse

Preparation time: 5 mins
Cooking time: 0 mins
Servings: 2
Ingredients
1/2 Cup Coconut Milk
1 Tsp. Maple Syrup
1-3 Tbsps. Cocoa Powder
Pinch Instant Coffee
2 Tbsps. Coconut Cream
Blackberries For Topping
Directions
Heat up coconut milk and maple syrup until it just begins to simmer.

Add cocoa and coffee in milk mixture.

Add cream to same mixture and whip until relatively stiff peaks form.

Transfer to a serving glass.

Chill the mousse in freezer for 2-3 hours.

Top with some berries and spoon of coconut cream.

Enjoy!

Nutrition: Protein: 3% 7 kcal Fat: 83% 163 kcal Carbohydrates: 13% 26 kcal

Coconut Rice With Mangos

Preparation time: 15 mins
Cooking time: 40 mins
Servings: 6
Ingredients
2 Cups Coconut Milk
1-1/2 Cups Coconut Flakes
1/4 Cup Maple Syrup
1 Mango Sliced

Directions
Heat saucepan over high heat.
Add coconut milk and bring it to boil.
Stir in coconut flakes and maple syrup.
Cover and cook on low heat for about 15 minutes or until liquid is completely dried.
Pour coconut rice in plate.
Serve with mango slice and enjoy.
Nutrition: Protein: 3% 8 kcal Fat: 69% 185 kcal Carbohydrates: 28% 75 kcal

Nori Snack Rolls

Preparation Time: 5 minutes
Cooking time: 10 minutes
Servings: 4 rolls
Ingredients
2 tablespoons almond, cashew, peanut, or others nut butter
2 tablespoons tamari, or soy sauce
4 standard nori sheets
1 mushroom, sliced
1 tablespoon pickled ginger
½ cup grated carrots
Directions
Preparing the Ingredients.
Preheat the oven to 350°F.

Mix together the nut butter and tamari until smooth and very thick. Lay out a nori sheet, rough side up, the long way.

Spread a thin line of the tamari mixture on the far end of the nori sheet, from side to side. Lay the mushroom slices, ginger, and carrots in a line at the other end (the end closest to you).

Fold the vegetables inside the nori, rolling toward the tahini mixture, which will seal the roll. Repeat to make 4 rolls.

Put on a baking sheet and bake for 8 to 10 minutes, or until the rolls are slightly browned and crispy at the ends. Let the rolls cool for a few minutes, then slice each roll into 3 smaller pieces.

Nutrition: Calories: 79; Total fat: 5g; Carbs: 6g; Fiber: 2g; Protein: 4g

Risotto Bites

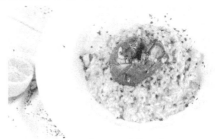

Preparation Time: 15 minutes
Cooking time: 20 minutes
Servings: 12 bites
Ingredients
½ cup panko bread crumbs
1 teaspoon paprika
1 teaspoon chipotle powder or ground cayenne pepper
1½ cups cold Green Pea Risotto
Nonstick cooking spray
Directions
Preparing the Ingredients.
Preheat the oven to 425°F.
Line a baking sheet with parchment paper.
On a large plate, combine the panko, paprika, and chipotle powder. Set aside.
Roll 2 tablespoons of the risotto into a ball.
Gently roll in the bread crumbs, and place on the prepared baking sheet. Repeat to make a total of 12 balls.
Spritz the tops of the risotto bites with nonstick cooking spray and bake for 15 to 20 minutes, until they begin to brown. Cool completely before storing in a large airtight container in a single layer (add a piece of parchment paper for a second layer) or in a plastic freezer bag.
Nutrition: Calories: 100; Fat: 2g; Protein: 6g; Carbohydrates: 17g; Fiber: 5g; Sugar: 2g; Sodium: 165 mg

Curried Tofu "Egg Salad" Pitas

Preparation Time: 15 minutes
Cooking time: 0 minutes
Servings: 4 sandwiches
Ingredients
1 pound extra-firm tofu, drained and patted dry
1/2 cup vegan mayonnaise, homemade or store-bought
1/4 cup chopped mango chutney, homemade or store-bought
2 teaspoons Dijon mustard
1 tablespoon hot or mild curry powder
1 teaspoon salt
1/8 teaspoon ground cayenne
¾ cup shredded carrots
2 celery ribs, minced
1/4 cup minced red onion
8 small Boston or other soft lettuce leaves
4 (7-inch) whole wheat pita breads, halved
Directions
Crumble the tofu and place it in a large bowl. Add the mayonnaise, chutney, mustard, curry powder, salt, and cayenne, and stir well until thoroughly mixed.
Add the carrots, celery, and onion and stir to combine. Refrigerate for 30 minutes to allow the flavors to blend.
Tuck a lettuce leaf inside each pita pocket, spoon some tofu mixture on top of the lettuce, and serve.

Tamari Toasted Almonds

Preparation Time: 2 minutes
Cooking time: 8 minutes
Servings: ½ cup
Ingredients
½ cup raw almonds, or sunflower seeds
2 tablespoons tamari, or soy sauce
1 teaspoon toasted sesame oil

Directions
Preparing the Ingredients.
Heat a dry skillet to medium-high heat, then add the almonds, stirring very frequently to keep them from burning. Once the almonds are toasted, 7 to 8 minutes for almonds, or 3 to 4 minutes for sunflower seeds, pour the tamari and sesame oil into the hot skillet and stir to coat.
You can turn off the heat, and as the almonds cool the tamari mixture will stick to and dry on the nuts.
Per Serving (1 tablespoon) Calories: 89; Total fat: 8g; Carbs: 3g; Fiber: 2g; Protein: 4g

Avocado And Tempeh Bacon Wraps

Preparation Time: 10 minutes
Cooking time: 8 minutes
Servings: 4 wraps
Ingredients
2 tablespoons olive oil
8 ounces tempeh bacon, homemade or store-bought
4 (10-inch) soft flour tortillas or lavash flatbread
1/4 cup vegan mayonnaise, homemade or store-bought
4 large lettuce leaves
2 ripe Hass avocados, pitted, peeled, and cut into 1/4-inch slices
1 large ripe tomato, cut into 1/4-inch slices
Directions
In a large skillet, heat the oil over medium heat. Add the tempeh bacon and cook until browned on both sides, about 8 minutes. Remove from the heat and set aside.

Place 1 tortilla on a work surface. Spread with some of the mayonnaise and one-fourth of the lettuce and tomatoes.

Pit, peel, and thinly slice the avocado and place the slices on top of the tomato. Add the reserved tempeh bacon and roll up tightly. Repeat with remaining Ingredients and serve.

Kale Chips

Preparation Time: 5 minutes
Cooking time: 25 minutes
Servings: 2
Ingredients
1 large bunch kale
1 tablespoon extra-virgin olive oil
½ teaspoon chipotle powder
½ teaspoon smoked paprika
¼ teaspoon salt

Directions
Preparing the Ingredients.
Preheat the oven to 275ºF.
Line a large baking sheet with parchment paper. In a large bowl, stem the kale and tear it into bite-size pieces. Add the olive oil, chipotle powder, smoked paprika, and salt.

Toss the kale with tongs or your hands, coating each piece well.

Spread the kale over the parchment paper in a single layer.

Bake for 25 minutes, turning halfway through, until crisp.

Cool for 10 to 15 minutes before dividing and storing in 2 airtight containers.

Nutrition: Calories: 144; Fat: 7g; Protein: 5g; Carbohydrates: 18g; Fiber: 3g; Sugar: 0g; Sodium: 363mg

Granola bars with Maple Syrup

Preparation time: 15 minutes
Cooking time: 0 minutes
Servings: 12
Ingredients
3/4 cup dates chopped
2 Tbsp chia seeds soaked
3/4 cup rolled oats
4 Tbsp Chopped nuts such Macadamia, almond, Brazilian...etc,
2 Tbsp shredded coconut
2 Tbsp pumpkin seeds
2 Tbsp sesame seeds
2 Tbsp hemp seeds
1/2 cup maple syrup (or to taste)
1/4 cup peanut butter
Directions:

Add all ingredients (except maple syrup and peanut butter) into a food processor and pulse just until roughly combined.

Add maple syrup and peanut butter and process until all ingredients are combined well.

Place baking paper onto a medium baking dish and spread the mixture.

Cover with a plastic wrap and press down to make it flat.

Chill granola in the fridge for one hour.

Cut it into 12 bars and serve.

Keep stored in an airtight container for up to 1 week.

Also, you can wrap them individually in parchment paper, and keep in the freezer in a large Ziploc bag.

Green Soy Beans Hummus

Preparation time: 15 minutes
Cooking time: 0 minutes
Servings: 6
Ingredients
1 1/2 cups frozen green soybeans
4 cups of water
coarse salt to taste
1/4 cup sesame paste
1/2 tsp grated lemon peel
3 Tbsp fresh lemon juice
2 cloves of garlic crushed
1/2 tsp ground cumin
1/4 tsp ground coriander
4 Tbsp extra virgin olive oil
1 Tbsp fresh parsley leaves chopped
Serving options: sliced cucumber, celery, olives
Directions:
1. In a saucepan, bring to boil 4 cups of water with 2 to 3 pinch of coarse salt.
2. Add in frozen soybeans, and cook for 5 minutes or until tender.
3. Rinse and drain soybeans into a colander.
4. Add soybeans and all remaining ingredients into a food processor.
5. Pulse until smooth and creamy.
6. Taste and adjust salt to taste.
7. Serve with sliced cucumber, celery, olives, bread...etc.

High Protein Avocado Guacamole

Preparation time: 15 minutes
Cooking time: 0 minutes
Servings: 4

Ingredients
1/2 cup of onion, finely chopped
1 chili pepper (peeled and finely chopped)
1 cup tomato, finely chopped
Cilantro leaves, fresh
2 avocados
2 Tbsp linseed oil
1/2 cup ground walnuts
1/2 lemon (or lime)
Salt
Directions:
Chop the onion, chili pepper, cilantro, and tomato; place in a large bowl.

Slice avocado, open vertically, and remove the pit.

Using the spoon take out the avocado flesh.

Mash the avocados with a fork and add into the bowl with onion mixture.

Add all remaining ingredients and stir well until ingredients combine well.

Taste and adjust salt and lemon/lime juice.

Keep refrigerated into covered glass bowl up to 5 days.

Homemade Energy Nut Bars

Preparation time: 15 minutes
Cooking time: 0 minutes
Servings: 4
Ingredients
1/2 cup peanuts
1 cup almonds
1/2 cup hazelnut, chopped
1 cup shredded coconut
1 cup almond butter
2 tsp sesame seeds toasted
1/2 cup coconut oil, freshly melted
2 Tbsp organic honey
1/4 tsp cinnamon
Directions
Add all nuts into a food processor and pulse for 1-2 minutes.

Add in shredded coconut, almond butter, sesame seeds, melted coconut oil, cinnamon, and honey; process only for one minute.

Cover a square plate/tray with parchment paper and apply the nut mixture.

Spread mixture vigorously with a spatula.
Place in the freezer for 4 hours or overnight.
Remove from the freezer and cut into rectangular bars.
Ready! Enjoy!

Honey Peanut Butter

Preparation time: 10 minutes
Cooking time: 0 minutes
Servings: 6
Ingredients
1 cup peanut butter
3/4 cup honey extracted
1/2 cup ground peanuts
1 tsp ground cinnamon
Directions:
Add all ingredients into your fast-speed blender, and blend until smooth.
Keep refrigerated.

Mediterranean Marinated Olives

Preparation time: 10 minutes
Cooking time: 0 minutes
Servings: 2
Ingredients
24 large olives, black, green, Kalamata
1/2 cup extra-virgin olive oil
4 cloves garlic, thinly sliced
2 Tbsp fresh lemon juice
2 tsp coriander seeds, crushed
1/2 tsp crushed red pepper
1 tsp dried thyme
1 tsp dried rosemary, crushed
Salt and ground pepper to taste
Directions:
Place olives and all remaining ingredients in a large container or bag, and shake to combine well.
Cover and refrigerate to marinate overnight.
Serve.
Keep refrigerated.

Nut Butter & Dates Granola

Preparation time: 1 hour
Cooking time: 55 minutes
Servings: 8
Ingredients
3 cups rolled oats
2 cups dates, pitted and chopped
1 cup flaked or shredded coconut
1/2 cup wheat germ
1/4 cup soy milk powder

1/2 cup almonds chopped
3/4 cup honey strained
1/2 cup almond butter (plain, unsalted) softened
1/4 cup peanut butter softened
Directions:
Preheat oven to 300F.
Add all ingredients into a food processor and pulse until roughly combined.
Spread mixture evenly into greased 10 x 15-inch baking pan.
Bake for 45 to 55 minutes.
Stir mixture several times during baking.
Remove from the oven and cool completely.
Store in a covered glass jar.

Oven-baked Caramelize Plantains

Preparation time: 30 minutes
Cooking time: 17 minutes
Servings: 4
Ingredients
4 medium plantains, peeled and sliced
2 Tbsp fresh orange juice
4 Tbsp brown sugar or to taste
1 Tbsp grated orange zest
4 Tbsp coconut butter, melted
Directions
Preheat oven to 360 F/180 C.
Place plantain slices in a heatproof dish.
Pour the orange juice over plantains, and then sprinkle with brown sugar and grated orange zest.
Melt coconut butter and pour evenly over plantains.
Cover with foil and bake for 15 to 17 minutes.
Serve warm or cold with honey or maple syrup.

Powerful Peas & Lentils Dip

Preparation time: 10 minutes
Cooking time: 0 minutes
Servings: 4
Ingredients
4 cups frozen peas
2 cup green lentils cooked
1 piece of grated ginger
1/2 cup fresh basil chopped
1 cup ground almonds
Juice of 1/2 lime
Pinch of salt
4 Tbsp sesame oil
1/4 cup Sesame seeds
Directions
Place all ingredients in a food processor or in a blender.
Blend until all ingredients combined well.
Keep refrigerated in an airtight container up to 4 days.

Protein "Raffaello" Candies

Preparation time: 15 minutes
Cooking time: 0 minutes
Servings: 12
Ingredients
1 1/2 cups desiccated coconut flakes
1/2 cup coconut butter softened
4 Tbsp coconut milk canned
4 Tbs coconut palm sugar (or granulated sugar)
1 tsp pure vanilla extract
1 Tbsp vegan protein powder (pea or soy)
15 whole almonds
Directions
Put 1 cup of desiccated coconut flakes, and all remaining ingredients in the blender (except almonds), and blend until soft.
If your dough is too thick, add some coconut milk.
In a bowl, add remaining coconut flakes.
Coat every almond in one tablespoon of mixture and roll into a ball.
Roll each ball in coconut flakes.
Chill in the fridge for several hours.

Protein-Rich Pumpkin Bowl

Preparation time: 10 minutes
Cooking time: 0 minutes
Servings: 2
Ingredients
1 1/2 cups almond milk (more or less depending on desired consistency)
1 cup pumpkin puree canned, with salt
1/2 cup chopped walnuts
1 scoop vegan soy protein powder
1 tsp pure vanilla extract
A handful of cacao nibs
Directions:
Add all ingredients in a blender apart from the cacao nibs.
Blend until smooth.
Serve in bowls and sprinkle with cacao nibs.

Savory Red Potato-Garlic Balls

Preparation time: 40 minutes
Cooking time: 25 minutes
Servings: 4
Ingredients
1 1/2 lbs of red potatoes
3 cloves of garlic finely chopped
1 Tbsp of fresh finely chopped parsley
1/4 tsp ground turmeric
Salt and ground pepper to taste
Directions:
Rinse potatoes and place unpeeled into a large pot.
Pour water to cover potatoes and bring to boil.
Cook for about 20 to 25 minutes on medium heat.
Rinse potatoes and let them cool down.
Peel potatoes and mash them; add finely chopped garlic, and the salt and pepper.
Form the potato mixture into small balls.
Sprinkle with chopped parsley and refrigerate for several hours.
Serve.

Spicy Smooth Red Lentil Dip

Preparation time: 35 minutes
Cooking time: 20 minutes
Servings: 4
Ingredients
1 cup red lentils
1 bay leaf
Sea salt to taste
2 garlic clove, finely chopped
2 Tbsp chopped cilantro leaves
1 Tbsp tomato paste
Lemon juice from 2 lemons, freshly squeezed
2 tsp ground cumin
4 Tbsp extra-virgin olive oil
Directions:

Rinse lentils and drain.

Combine lentils and bay leaf in a medium saucepan.

Pour enough water to cover lentils completely, and bring to boil.

Cover tightly, reduce heat to medium, and simmer for about 20 minutes.

Season salt to taste, and stir well. Note: Always season with the salt after cooking – if salt is added before, the lentils will become tough.

Drain the lentils in a colander. Discard the bay leaf and let the lentils cool for 10 minutes.

Transfer the lentils to a food processor and add all remaining ingredients.

Pulse until all ingredients combined well.

Taste and adjust seasonings if needed.

Transfer a lentil dip into a glass container and refrigerate at least 2 hours before serving.

Steamed Broccoli with Sesame

Preparation time: 15 minutes
Cooking time: 5 minutes
Servings: 2
Ingredients
1 1/2 lb fresh broccoli florets
1/2 cup sesame oil
4 Tbsp sesame seeds
Salt and ground pepper to taste
Directions:
Place broccoli florets in a steamer basket above boiling water.

Cover and steam for about 4 to 5 minutes.

Remove from steam and place broccoli in serving the dish.

Season with the salt and pepper, and drizzle with sesame oil; toss to coat.

Sprinkle with sesame seeds and serve immediately.

Vegan Eggplant Patties

Preparation time: 30 minutes
Cooking time: 15 minutes
Servings: 6
Ingredients
2 big eggplants
1 onion finely diced
1 Tbsp smashed garlic cloves
1 bunch raw parsley, chopped
1/2 cup almond meal
4 Tbsp Kalamata olives, pitted and sliced
1 Tbsp baking soda
Salt and ground pepper to taste

Olive oil or avocado oil, for frying
Directions
Peel off eggplants, rinse, and cut in half.

Sauté eggplant cubes in a non-stick skillet - occasionally stirring - about 10 minutes.

Transfer to a large bowl and mash with an immersion blender.

Add eggplant puree into a bowl and add in all remaining ingredients (except oil).

Knead a mixture using your hands until the dough is smooth, sticky, and easy to shape.

Shape mixture into 6 patties.

Heat the olive oil in a frying skillet on medium-high heat.

Fry patties for about 3 to 4 minutes per side.

Remove patties on a platter lined with kitchen paper towel to drain.

Serve warm.

Vegan Breakfast Sandwich

Preparation Time: 10minutes
Cooking Time: 10 minutes
Servings: 3
Ingredients
1 tsp. coconut oil
6 slices of bread
1 14 oz container
1-2 tsp. vegan extra firm tofu mayo
1 tsp. turmeric
1 cup of greens
1/2 tsp. garlic
1-2 medium powder tomatoes
1/2 tsp. Kala
6 pickle slices
Namak (black Fresh cracked salt) pepper
3 melty vegan cheese slices
Directions:
Season one facet of the tofu with salt, garlic powder, break up pepper, and turmeric. I just 15

sprinkled it out of the flavor bins. You will season the second side within the field when it is a perfect possibility to flip them.

In a medium skillet, warmth oil over medium warmth and notice the tofu cuts organized aspect down on the dish. While the bottom facet is cooking, season the pinnacle side. Let the tofu cook dinner for three to 5 minutes, till marginally darker and clean. Presently turn the cuts over and fry the alternative aspect for 3-5 minutes. Presently's a respectable time to pop the bread in the toaster, on every occasion liked.

To liquefy the cheddar, on a preparing sheet, place 2 cuts of tofu one next to the opposite, with a reduce of cheddar over every set. Put it within the broiler on prepare dinner for 1-three minutes, until the cheddar is dissolved. You can likewise utilize a toaster broiler.

Spread mayo on the two aspects of the bread.

Spot the two cuts of tofu with cheddar on one aspect. Include the vegetables and tomatoes.

Presently include several pickle cuts and near the sandwich collectively. Cut nook to corner

Chickpea And Mushroom Burger

Preparation Time: 20minutes
Cooking Time: 16 minutes
Serving: 4
Ingredients
240g chickpeas
Half tsp. sea salt
2 level tsp. gram
Half medium-flour
1 small red sized apple
1 tsp. dried onion
parsley
2 large cloves
1 tsp. fresh garlic
75g tasty rosemary
1 medium-sized mushrooms tomato
1 tsp. tahini

Directions
Pulverize garlic, diced onion and slash the mushrooms into little pieces; saute together in a search for a gold couple of moments.

Generally, pound chickpeas in an enormous blending bowl in with a potato masher or fork. The pound doesn't need to be absolutely smooth, in spite of the fact that you do need to give it a decent squeezing through with the goal that a great deal of it is very soft. It's fine to leave a couple of provincial looking pieces.

Mesh the half apple.

Include the gram flour, tahini, salt, and apple and combine all utilizing the rear of a metal spoon

Finely cleave the rosemary and slash the tomato into little pieces.

Include the sauteed things alongside every single residual ingredient into a bowl, pushing down and blending completely with a metal spoon.

Partition into 4 and solidly shape and form into patties.

Spot onto a barbecue plate and warmth under a medium flame broil for roughly 8 minutes on each side.

Apple Raspberry Cobbler

Preparation Time: 50 minutes
Servings: 4
A safer type of fruit cobbler where a cut in sugar enhances the fruit.
Ingredients
3 apples, peeled, cored, and chopped
2 tbsp pure date sugar
1 cup fresh raspberries
2 tbsp unsalted plant butter
½ cup whole-wheat flour
1 cup toasted rolled oats
2 tbsp pure date sugar
1 tsp cinnamon powder

Directions

Preheat the oven to 350 F and grease a baking dish with some plant butter.

Add the apples, date sugar, and 3 tbsp of water to a medium pot. Cook over low heat until the date sugar melts and then, mix in the raspberries. Cook until the fruits soften, 10 minutes.

Pour and spread the fruit mixture into the baking dish and set aside.

In a blender, add the plant butter, flour, oats, date sugar, and cinnamon powder. Pulse a few times until crumbly.

Spoon and spread the mixture on the fruit mix until evenly layered.

Bake in the oven for 25 to 30 minutes or until golden brown on top.

Remove the dessert, allow cooling for 2 minutes, and serve.

Nutritional info per serving

Calories 539 | Fats 12g| Carbs 105.7g | Protein 8.2g

White Chocolate Pudding

Preparation Time: 4 hours 20 minutes
Servings: 4
Ingredients
3 tbsp flax seed + 9 tbsp water
3 tbsp cornstarch
¼ tbsp salt
1 cup cashew cream
2 ½ cups almond milk
½ pure date sugar
1 tbsp vanilla caviar
6 oz unsweetened white chocolate chips
Whipped coconut cream for topping
Sliced bananas and raspberries for topping
Directions

In a small bowl, mix the flax seed powder with water and allow thickening for 5 minutes to make the flax egg.

In a large bowl, whisk the cornstarch and salt, and then slowly mix in the in the cashew cream until smooth. Whisk in the flax egg until well combined.

Pour the almond milk into a pot and whisk in the date sugar. Cook over medium heat while frequently stirring until the sugar dissolves. Reduce the heat to low and simmer until steamy and bubbly around the edges.

Pour half of the almond milk mixture into the flax egg mix, whisk well and pour this mixture into the remaining milk content in the pot. Whisk continuously until well combined.

Bring the new mixture to a boil over medium heat while still frequently stirring and scraping all the corners of the pot, 2 minutes.

Turn the heat off, stir in the vanilla caviar, then the white chocolate chips until melted. Spoon the mixture into a bowl, allow cooling for 2 minutes, cover with plastic wraps making sure to press the plastic onto the surface of the pudding, and refrigerate for 4 hours.

Remove the pudding from the fridge, take off the plastic wrap and whip for about a minute.

Spoon the dessert into serving cups, swirl some coconut whipping cream on top, and top with the bananas and raspberries. Enjoy immediately.

Nutritional info per serving

Calories 654 | Fats 47.9g| Carbs 52.1g | Protein 7.3g

Ambrosia Salad With Pecans

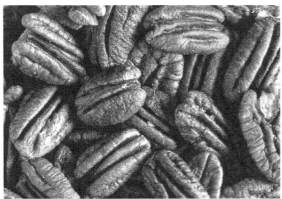

Preparation Time: 15 minutes + 1 hour chilling
Servings: 4

These are the ingredients that inflict anguish if skipped at the celebration plate.

Ingredients
1 cup pure coconut cream
½ tsp vanilla extract

2 medium bananas, peeled and cut into chunks
1 ½ cups unsweetened coconut flakes
4 tbsp toasted pecans, chopped
1 cup pineapple tidbits, drained
1 (11 oz) can mandarin oranges, drained
¾ cup maraschino cherries, stems removed
Directions
In medium bowl, mix the coconut cream and vanilla extract until well combined.

In a larger bowl, combine the bananas, coconut flakes, pecans, pineapple, oranges, and cherries until evenly distributed.

Pour on the coconut cream mixture and fold well into the salad.

Chill in the refrigerator for 1 hour and serve afterwards.

Nutritional info per serving
Calories 648 | Fats 36g| Carbs 85.7g | Protein 6.6g

Peanut Butter Blossom Biscuits

Preparation Time: 15 minutes + 1 hour chilling
Servings: 4
Ingredients
1 tbsp flax seed powder + 3 tbsp water
1 cup pure date sugar + more for dusting
½ cup creamy peanut butter
1 tsp vanilla extract
1 ¾ cup whole-wheat flour
1 tsp baking soda
¼ tsp salt
¼ cup unsweetened chocolate chips
Directions
In a small bowl, mix the flax seed powder with water and allow thickening for 5 minutes to make the flax egg.

In a medium bowl using an electric mixer, whisk the date sugar, plant butter, and peanut butter until light and fluffy.

Mix in the flax egg and vanilla until well combined. Add the flour, baking soda, salt, and whisk well again.

Fold in the chocolate chips, cover the bowl with a plastic wrap, and refrigerate for 1 hour. After, preheat the oven to 375 F and line a baking sheet with parchment paper.

Use a cookie sheet to scoop mounds of the batter onto the sheet with 1-inch intervals. Bake in the oven for 9 to 10 minutes or until golden brown and slightly cracked on top.

Remove the cookies from the oven, cool for 3 minutes, roll in some date sugar, and serve.

Nutritional info per serving
Calories 839 | Fats 52.5g| Carbs 77.9g | Protein 21.1g

Chocolate & Almond Butter Barks

Preparation Time: 35 minutes
Servings: 4
Chewy fluffy almonds is equal to delicious almond bark, handmade dairy-free chocolate bars!
Ingredients
1/3 cup coconut oil, melted
¼ cup almond butter, melted
2 tbsp unsweetened coconut flakes.
1 tsp pure maple syrup
A pinch ground rock salt
¼ cup unsweetened cocoa nibs

Directions
Line a baking tray with baking paper and set aside.

In a medium bowl, mix the coconut oil, almond butter, coconut flakes, maple syrup, and then fold in the rock salt and cocoa nibs.

Pour and spread the mixture on the baking sheet, chill in the refrigerator for 20 minutes or until firm.

Remove the dessert, break into shards and enjoy immediately.

Preserve extras in the refrigerator.

Nutritional info per serving
Calories 279 | Fats 28.1g| Carbs 8.6g | Protein 4.4g

Mini Berry Tarts

Preparation Time: 35 minutes + 1 hour chilling
Servings: 4
Tickle-sized berries-filled with surprises, oh so delicious! Also so delicious that you can't stop having them.
Ingredients
For the piecrust:

4 tbsp flax seed powder + 12 tbsp water
1/3 cup whole-wheat flour + more for dusting
½ tsp salt
¼ cup plant butter, cold and crumbled
3 tbsp pure malt syrup
1 ½ tsp vanilla extract
For the filling:
6 oz cashew cream
6 tbsp pure date sugar
¾ tsp vanilla extract
1 cup mixed frozen berries
Directions
Preheat the oven to 350 F and grease a mini pie pans with cooking spray.

In a medium bowl, mix the flax seed powder with water and allow soaking for 5 minutes.

In a large bowl, combine the flour and salt. Add the butter and using an electric hand mixer, whisk until crumbly. Pour in the flax egg, malt syrup, vanilla, and mix until smooth dough forms.

Flatten the dough on a flat surface, cover with plastic wrap, and refrigerate for 1 hour.

After, lightly dust a working surface with some flour, remove the dough onto the surface, and using a rolling pin, flatten the dough into a 1-inch diameter circle,

Use a large cookie cutter, cut out rounds of the dough and fit into the pie pans. Use a knife to trim the edges of the pan. Lay a parchment paper on the dough cups, pour on some baking beans and bake in the oven until golden brown, 15 to 20 minutes.

Remove the pans from the oven, pour out the baking beans, and allow cooling.

In a medium bowl, mix the cashew cream, date sugar, and vanilla extract.

Divide the mixture into the tart cups and top with berries. Serve immediately.

Nutritional info per serving
Calories 545 | Fats 33.5g| Carbs 53.6g | Protein 10.6g

Mixed Nut Chocolate Fudge

Preparation Time: 2 hours 10 minutes
Servings: 4
A recipe for chocolate fudge that takes just 10 minutes to make and requires ingredients that are readily available.
Ingredients
3 cups unsweetened chocolate chips
¼ cup thick coconut milk
1 ½ tsp vanilla extract
A pinch salt

1 cup chopped mixed nuts

Directions
Line a 9-inch square pan with baking paper and set aside.

Melt the chocolate chips, coconut milk, and vanilla in a medium pot over low heat.

Mix in the salt and nuts until well distributed and pour the mixture into the square pan.

Refrigerate for at least for at least 2 hours.

Remove from the fridge, cut into squares and serve.

Nutritional info per serving
Calories 907 | Fats 31.5g| Carbs 152.1g | Protein 7.7g

Date Cake Slices

Preparation Time: 1 hour 20 minutes
Servings: 4
With a slightly thick yet fluffy texture, they're super soft.
Ingredients
½ cup cold plant butter, cut in pieces, plus extra for greasing
1 tbsp flax seed powder + 3 tbsp water
½ cup whole-wheat flour, plus extra for dusting
¼ cup chopped pecans and walnuts
1 tsp baking powder
1 tsp baking soda
1 tsp cinnamon powder
1 tsp salt
1/3 cup water
1/3 cup pitted dates, chopped
½ cup pure date sugar
1 tsp vanilla extract
¼ cup pure date syrup for drizzling.
Directions
Preheat the oven to 350 F and lightly grease a round baking dish with some plant butter.

In a small bowl, mix the flax seed powder with water and allow thickening for 5 minutes to make the flax egg.

In a food processor, add the flour, nuts, baking powder, baking soda, cinnamon powder, and salt. Blend until well combined.

Add the water, dates, date sugar, and vanilla. Process until smooth with tiny pieces of dates evident.

Pour the batter into the baking dish and bake in the oven for 1 hour and 10 minutes or until a toothpick inserted comes out clean. Remove the dish from the oven, invert the cake onto a serving platter to cool, drizzle with the date syrup, slice, and serve.

Nutritional info per serving

Calories 850 | Fats 61.2g| Carbs 65.7g | Protein 12.8g

Chocolate Mousse Cake

Preparation Time: 40 minutes + 6 hours 30 minutes chilling

Servings: 4

Have a cake with a basic mousse of chocolate and tell me how you feel.

Ingredients

2/3 cup toasted almond flour

¼ cup unsalted plant butter, melted

2 cups unsweetened chocolate bars, broken into pieces

2 ½ cups coconut cream

Fresh raspberries or strawberries for topping

Directions

Lightly grease a 9-inch springform pan with some plant butter and set aside.

Mix the almond flour and plant butter in a medium bowl and pour the mixture into the springform pan. Use the spoon to spread and press the mixture into the bottom of the pan. Place in the refrigerator to firm for 30 minutes.

Meanwhile, pour the chocolate in a safe microwave bowl and melt for 1 minute stirring every 30 seconds.

Remove from the microwave and mix in the coconut cream and maple syrup.

Remove the cake pan from the oven, pour the chocolate mixture on top making to sure to shake the pan and even the layer. Chill further for 4 to 6 hours.

Take out the pan from the fridge, release the cake and garnish with the raspberries or strawberries.

Slice and serve.

Nutritional info per serving

Calories 608 | Fats 60.5g| Carbs 19.8g | Protein 6.3g

Apricot Tarte Tatin

Preparation Time: 30 minutes + 1 hour chilling

Servings: 4

The fruit variety is the best overall, but it also goes well with apricots – happiness on a table.

Ingredients

For the piecrust:

4 tbsp flax seed powder + 12 tbsp water

¼ cup almond flour + extra for dusting

3 tbsp whole-wheat flour

½ tsp salt

¼ cup plant butter, cold and crumbled

3 tbsp pure maple syrup

1 ½ tsp vanilla extract

For the filling:

4 tbsp melted plant butter + more for brushing

3 tsp pure maple syrup

1 tsp vanilla extract

1 lemon, juiced

12 apricots, halved and pitted

½ cup coconut cream

3 to 4 fresh basil leaves to garnish

Directions

Preheat the oven to 350 F and grease a large pie pan with cooking spray.

In a medium bowl, mix the flax seed powder with water and allow thickening for 5 minutes.

In a large bowl, combine the flours and salt. Add the plant butter and using an electric hand mixer, whisk until crumbly. Pour in the flax egg, maple syrup, vanilla, and mix until smooth dough forms. Flatten the dough on a flat surface, cover with plastic wrap, and refrigerate for 1 hour.

After, lightly dust a working surface with almond flour, remove the dough onto the surface, and using a rolling pin, flatten the dough into a 1-inch diameter circle. Set aside.

In a large bowl, mix the plant butter, maple syrup, vanilla, and lemon juice. Add the apricots to the mixture and coat well.

Arrange the apricots (open side down) in the pie pan and lay the dough on top. Press to fit and cut off the dough hanging on the edges. Brush the top with more plant butter and bake in the oven for 35 to 40 minutes or until golden brown, and puffed up.

Remove the pie pan from the oven, allow cooling for 5 minutes, and run a butter knife around the edges of the pastry. Invert the dessert onto a large plate, spread the coconut cream on top, and garnish with the basil leaves. Slice and serve.

Nutritional info per serving

Calories 484 | Fats 33.8g| Carbs 46.4g | Protein 2.8g

Chocolate & Pistachio Popsicles

Preparation Time: 5 minutes + 3 hours chilling
Servings: 4

A popsicle is one of those wonders full of endless possibilities that are creative and mouth-watering.

Ingredients
½ cup unsweetened chocolate chips, melted
1 ½ cups oat milk
1 tbsp unsweetened cocoa powder
3 tbsp pure date syrup
1 tsp vanilla extract
A handful pistachios, chopped

Directions

In a blender, add chocolate, oat milk, cocoa powder, date syrup, vanilla, pistachios, and process until smooth. Divide the mixture into popsicle molds and freeze for 3 hours.

Dip the popsicle molds in warm water to loosen the popsicles and pull out the popsicles.

Nutritional info per serving
Calories 315 | Fats 17.8g| Carbs 34.9g | Protein 11.9g

Strawberry Cupcakes With Cashew Cheese Frosting

Preparation Time: 35 minutes + 30 minutes chilling

Servings: 4

To make this lovely pink ganache, you just need three basic ingredients. With freshly strawberry puree, it takes on a buttery flavor.

Ingredients
For the cupcakes:
2 cups whole-wheat flour
¼ cup cornstarch
2 ½ tsp baking powder
1 ½ cups pure date sugar
½ tsp salt
¾ cup unsalted plant butter, room temperature
3 tsp vanilla extract
1 cup strawberries, pureed
1 cup oat milk, room temperature
For the frosting:
¾ cup cashew cream
2 tbsp coconut oil, melted
3 tbsp pure maple syrup
1 tsp vanilla extract
1 tsp freshly squeezed lemon juice
¼ tsp salt
2-4 tbsp water as needed for blending

Directions

Preheat the oven to 350 F and line a 12-holed muffin tray with cupcake liners. Set aside.

In a large bowl, mix the flour, cornstarch, baking powder, date sugar, and salt.

Using an electric mixer, whisk in the plant butter, vanilla extract, strawberries, and oat milk until well combined.

Divide the mixture into the muffin cups two-thirds way up and bake in the oven for 20 to 25 minutes or until golden brown on top and a toothpick inserted comes out clean. Remove the cupcakes and allow cooling while you make the frosting.

In a blender, add the cashew cream, coconut oil, maple syrup, vanilla, lemon juice, and salt. Process until smooth. If the mixture is too thick, add some water to lighten the consistency a little. Pour the frosting into medium and chill for 30 minutes.

Transfer the mixture into a piping bag and swirl mounds of the frosting onto the cupcakes. Serve immediately.

Nutritional info per serving
Calories 853 | Fats 42g| Carbs 112.8g | Protein 14.3g

Nut Stuffed Sweet Apples

Preparation Time: 35 minutes
Servings: 4
This nut Stuffed Baked Apples are a buzz-friendly sliding dessert, or say, one or two weekend desserts snack.

Ingredients
4 gala apples
3 tbsp pure maple syrup
4 tbsp almond flour
6 tbsp pure date sugar
6 tbsp plant butter, cold and cubed
1 cup chopped mixed nuts
Directions
Preheat the oven the 400 F.

Slice off the top of the apples and use a melon baller or spoon to scoop out the cores of the apples. In a bowl, mix the maple syrup, almond flour, date sugar, butter, and nuts.

Spoon the mixture into the apples and then bake in the oven for 25 minutes or until the nuts are golden brown on top and the apples soft. Remove the apples from the oven, allow cooling, and serve.

Nutritional info per serving
Calories 581 | Fats 43.6g| Carbs 52.1g | Protein 3.6g

Classic Pecan Pie

Preparation Time: 50 minutes + 1 hour chilling
Servings: 4
The traditional pie is baked to a lustrous brown pecan load.

Ingredients
For the piecrust:
4 tbsp flax seed powder + 12 tbsp water
1/3 cup whole-wheat flour + more for dusting
½ tsp salt
¼ cup plant butter, cold and crumbled
3 tbsp pure malt syrup
1 ½ tsp vanilla extract
For the filling:

3 tbsp flax seed powder + 9 tbsp water
2 cups toasted pecans, coarsely chopped
1 cup light corn syrup
½ cup pure date sugar
1 tbsp pure pomegranate molasses
4 tbsp plant butter, melted
½ tsp salt
2 tsp vanilla extract
Directions
Preheat the oven to 350 F and grease a large pie pan with cooking spray.

In a medium bowl, mix the flax seed powder with water and allow thickening for 5 minutes. Do this for the filling's flax egg too in a separate bowl.

In a large bowl, combine the flour and salt. Add the plant butter and using an electric hand mixer, whisk until crumbly. Pour in the crust's flax egg, maple syrup, vanilla, and mix until smooth dough forms.

Flatten the dough on a flat surface, cover with plastic wrap, and refrigerate for 1 hour.

After, lightly dust a working surface with flour, remove the dough onto the surface, and using a rolling pin, flatten the dough into a 1-inch diameter circle.

Lay the dough on the pie pan and press to fit the shape of the pan. Use a knife to trim the edges of the pan. Lay a parchment paper on the dough, pour on some baking beans and bake in the oven until golden brown, 15 to 20 minutes. Remove the pan from the oven, pour out the baking beans, and allow cooling.

In a large bowl, mix the filling's flax egg, pecans, corn syrup, date sugar, pomegranate molasses, plant butter, salt, and vanilla. Pour and spread the mixture on the piecrust. Bake further for 20 minutes or until the filling sets. Remove from the oven, decorate with more pecans, slice, and cool. Slice and serve.

Nutritional info per serving
Calories 992 | Fats 59.8g| Carbs 117.6 g | Protein 8g

Summer Banana Pudding

Preparation Time: 25 minutes + 1 hour
Servings: 4
It's a no bake dessert that's perfect for a group's last minute get together. Just that something that everyone loves!
Ingredients
1 cup unsweetened almond milk
2 cups cashew cream
¾ cup + 1 tbsp pure date sugar

¼ tsp salt
3 tbsp cornstarch
2 tbsb cold plant butter, cut into 4 pieces
1 tsp vanilla extract
2 medium banana, peeled and sliced

Directions

In a medium pot, mix the almond milk, cashew cream, date sugar, and salt. Cook over medium heat until slightly thickened, 10 to 15 minutes.

Stir in the cornstarch, plant butter, vanilla extract, and banana extract. Cook further for 1 to 2 minutes or until the pudding thickens. Dish the pudding into 4 serving bowls and chill in the refrigerator for at least 1 hour. To serve, top with the bananas and enjoy!

Nutritional info per serving

Calories 466 | Fats 29.9g| Carbs 47.8g | Protein 4.3g

Cranberry Truffles

Preparation Time: 15 minutes
Servings: 4
Of sweet little cranberry pops, these cranberry truffles are creamy. They're a tasty little surprise and they make a really cute present.

Ingredients
2 cups fresh cranberries
2 tbsp pure date syrup
1 tsp vanilla extract
16 oz cashew cream
4 tbsp plant butter
3 tbsp unsweetened cocoa powder
2 tbsp pure date sugar

Directions
Set a silicone egg tray aside.
Puree the cranberries, date syrup, and vanilla in a blender until smooth.
Add the cashew cream and plant butter to a medium pot. Heat over medium heat until the mixture is well combined. Turn the heat off.

Mix in the cranberry mixture and divide the mixture into the muffin holes. Refrigerate for 40 minutes or until firm.

Remove the tray and pop out the truffles.

Meanwhile, mix the cocoa powder and date sugar on a plate. Roll the truffles in the mixture until well dusted and serve.

Nutritional info per serving

Calories 882 | Fats 66.35g| Carbs 64.5g | Protein 19.95g

Mango & Lemon Cheesecake

Preparation Time: 20 minutes + 3 hours 30 minutes   chilling
Servings: 4
This No Bake Mango Cheesecake is a love treat perfect and delicious!
Ingredients
2/3 cup toasted rolled oats
¼ cup plant butter, melted
3 tbsp pure date sugar
6 oz cashew cream cheese
¼ cup coconut milk
1 lemon, zested and lemon juiced
¼ cup just-boiled water
3 tsp agar agar powder
1 large ripe mangoes, peeled and chopped

Directions

Process the oats, butter, and date sugar in a blender until smooth.

Pour the mixture into a greased 9-inch springform pan and press the mixture onto the bottom of the pan. Refrigerate for 30 minutes until firm while you make the filling.

In a large bowl, using an electric mixer, whisk the cashew cream cheese until smooth. Beat in the coconut milk, lemon zest, and lemon juice.

Mix the boiled water and agar agar powder until dissolved and whisk this mixture into the creamy mix. Fold in the mangoes.

Remove the cake pan from the fridge and pour in the mango mixture. Shake the pan to ensure a smooth layering on top. Refrigerate further for at least 3 hours.

Remove the cheesecake from the fridge, release the cake pan, slice, and serve.

Nutritional info per serving

Calories 337 | Fats 28g| Carbs 21.3g | Protein 5.4g

Plum Cashew Cheesecake

Preparation Time: 20 minutes + 3 hours 30 minutes   chilling
Servings: 4

Cheesecake is the favorite of most people and combined with cashew and plum, excellency is bestowed on us.

Ingredients

2/3 cup toasted rolled oats

¼ cup plant butter, melted

3 tbsp pure date sugar

6 oz cashew cream cheese

¼ cup oats milk

¼ cup just-boiled water

3 tsp agar agar powder

4 plums, cored and finely diced

2 tbsp toasted cashew nuts, chopped

Directions

Process the oats, butter, and date sugar in a blender until smooth.

Pour the mixture into a greased 9-inch springform pan and press the mixture onto the bottom of the pan. Refrigerate for 30 minutes until firm while you make the filling.

In a large bowl, using an electric mixer, whisk the cashew cream cheese until smooth. Beat in the oats milk.

Mix the boiled water and agar agar powder until dissolved and whisk this mixture into the creamy mix. Fold in the plums.

Remove the cake pan from the fridge and pour in the plum mixture. Shake the pan to ensure a smooth layering on top. Refrigerate further for at least 3 hours.

Take out the cake pan, release the cake, and garnish with the cashew nuts.

Slice and serve.

Nutritional info per serving

Calories 354 | Fats 26.7g| Carbs 27.7g | Protein 6.4g

Matcha Cheesecake

Preparation Time: 20 minutes + 3 hours 30 minutes   chilling
Servings: 4

This is a soft and simple cheesecake with green tea powder included to give it an extra yummy taste!

Ingredients

2/3 cup toasted rolled oats

¼ cup plant butter, melted

3 tbsp pure date sugar

6 oz cashew cream cheese

¼ cup almond milk

1 tbsp matcha powder

¼ cup just-boiled water

3 tsp agar agar powder

2 tbsp toasted hazelnuts, chopped

Directions

Process the oats, butter, and date sugar in a blender until smooth.

Pour the mixture into a greased 9-inch springform pan and press the mixture onto the bottom of the pan. Refrigerate for 30 minutes until firm while you make the filling.

In a large bowl, using an electric mixer, whisk the cashew cream cheese until smooth. Beat in the almond milk and mix in the matcha powder until smooth.

Mix the boiled water and agar agar until dissolved and whisk this mixture into the creamy mix. Fold in the hazelnuts until well distributed.

Remove the cake pan from the fridge and pour in the cream mixture. Shake the pan to ensure a smooth layering on top. Refrigerate further for at least 3 hours.

Take out the cake pan, release the cake, slice, and serve.

Nutritional info per serving

Calories 650 | Fats 59.33g| Carbs 25.84g | Protein 13.54g

Brown Butter Pumpkin Pie

Preparation Time: 1 hour 10 minutes + 1 hour chilling

Servings: 4

Give it a try when you want to use your own fresh pumpkin or squash.

Ingredients

For the piecrust:

4 tbsp flax seed powder + 12 tbsp water

1/3 cup whole-wheat flour

½ tsp salt

¼ cup plant butter, cold and crumbled

3 tbsp pure malt syrup

1 ½ tsp vanilla extract

For the filling:

2 tbsp flax seed powder + 6 tbsp water

4 tbsp plant butter

¼ cup pure maple syrup

¼ cup pure date sugar

1 tsp cinnamon powder

½ tsp ginger powder

1/8 tsp cloves powder

¼ tsp salt

1 (15 oz) can pumpkin purée

1 cup almond milk

Directions

Preheat the oven to 350 F. In a bowl, mix flax seed powder with water and allow thickening for 5 minutes. Do this for the filling's flax egg too in a separate bowl. In a bowl, combine the and salt. Add in plant butter and whisk until crumbly. Pour in the crust's flax egg, maple syrup, vanilla, and mix until smooth dough forms. Flatten the dough on a flat surface, cover with plastic wrap, and refrigerate for 1 hour.

After, lightly dust a working surface with flour, remove the dough onto the surface, and using a rolling pin, flatten the dough into a 1-inch diameter circle. Lay the dough on a greased pie pan and press to fit the shape of the pan. Use a knife to trim the edges of the pan. Lay a parchment paper on the dough, pour on some baking beans and bake for 15-20 minutes. Remove, pour out the baking beans, and allow cooling.

In a bowl, whisk filling's flax seed, butter, maple syrup, date sugar, cinnamon powder, ginger powder, cloves powder, salt, pumpkin purée, and almond milk. Pour the mixture onto the piecrust and bake further for 35-40 minutes. Slice and serve afterwards.

Nutritional info per serving

Calories 544 | Fats 31g| Carbs 58.4g | Protein 9.8g

Vegan Cheese

What is Vegan Cheese, and Why Are People going Nuts for it?

You may have seen some vegan cheeses in your local grocery stores and wonder, "Is it possible to make cheese without milk?"

With creative vegans trying to find an alternative to daily food items, countless cheese recipes have been done. There is now a wide selection of dairy-free cheeses in the market and recipes people enjoy.

Vegan cheese is a substitute for the conventional cheese people have grown eating. They're made with non-dairy or plant-based ingredients. Most consumers who buy and eat this type of cheese are vegan, but there are those who simply don't want to consume animal products for health reasons.

Vegan cheeses were first sold commercially in the 1980s. Back then, they weren't as popular as they are now. The first vegan cheeses sold usually tasted bad and had an obvious artificial texture.

Nowadays, vegan cheeses have evolved into something that can compete with commercial dairy cheeses. They taste better and have a texture closer to dairy cheese.

Many vegan cheeses use nuts as a base. They're packed with health benefits and contain fiber, minerals, and probiotics. There are also alternatives for people who have nut allergies.

One more thing that attracts people to consume vegan cheese is the wide array of vegan cheese recipes that are easy to do.

Different Types of Vegan Cheese Bases

Before trying any of the recipes in this book, you'll have to know the different bases of vegan cheese. This will help you determine what kind of vegan cheese you can make and enjoy at home.

Here are the ingredients used as a base for vegan cheese:

Seeds And Nuts

These are the most commonly used base for homemade vegan cheese.

Seeds and nuts are often soaked, processed, or fermented when used for making dairy-free cheeses. These ingredients taste bland on their own, meaning adding and combining flavors remains easy.

The nuts and seeds most often used for vegan cheese recipes are:

- Cashews
- Macadamia
- Almonds
- Sunflower seeds
- Pumpkin seeds

Soy

Commercial vegan cheeses are commonly soy-based. Soy products are used because they have the closest characteristics to real cheese.

Tofu may be the most widely used form of soy protein for vegan cheese. Both soft or silken and firm tofu can become different types of soft and hard cheeses. Tofu is blander than nuts, so achieving a cheese-like taste is definitely possible.

Soy is sometimes combined with a milk protein called casein. This protein allows the resulting cheese to have a melty characteristic, just like the real thing. But, to be perfectly clear, cheeses with casein aren't considered vegan.

What's a bit worrying though, is that some commercial cheeses labeled as vegan or vegetarian actually contain small amounts of the milk protein.

Flour

More often, flour is only a supplementary ingredient to other vegan cheese bases. But, there are some recipes that use flour as the base. Flour is usually used to create vegan cheese sauces though.

Some of the popular starchy flours used for vegan cheese recipes are:

- Tapioca starch/flour
- All-purpose flour
- Potato starch/flour
- Arrowroot flour

Vegetables

Some vegan cheeses have root vegetables as the base. The most common vegetables used are carrots and potatoes. Cheeses which use these as bases often have a soft and saucy consistency.

Non-Dairy Milk

Vegan cheese can also have non-dairy or plant-based milk as a base. It doesn't have casein like animal's milk, so vegan cheeses couldn't mimic the melty quality of real cheese. Other ingredients can be added, however, to somehow make the cruelty-free alternative a bit more similar.

Solidified Vegetable Oils

One of the things that people love about cheese is the creaminess. Some vegan cheeses use vegetable oils which are naturally loaded with fat, making it possible to copy the creaminess of real cheese. But, oils alone cannot serve as a base. Other ingredients like starch, flour, and agar-agar powder are used to create cheeses with vegetable oils.

Nut Milk

Seed-Free, Soy-Free

Making homemade Nut Milk is incredibly easy to do and yields a product far more delicious than buying it from the store. The process is the same for all nut and seed milks, but the soaking time varies. After you make Nut Milk a few times, it will be your new normal and set the foundation for so many other dairy-free recipes, especially vegan cheese!

Preparation time: 12 hours
Cooking time: 0 minutes
Servings: 4 to 6 cups
Active time: 12 minutes
Inactive Time: Varies, depending on nut soaking time
Ingredients
1 cup nuts (cashews, almonds, or walnuts)
4 to 6 cups filtered water

Directions:

In a small bowl, soak the nuts in water for the required time (8 to 12 hours for almonds or 6 to 12 hours for cashews and walnuts). Drain and rinse the nuts.

In a high-speed blender, combine the nuts with 4 to 6 cups of filtered water, depending on how creamy or thin you'd like the milk to be.

Blend for 2 minutes on high and then pour through a nut milk bag or cheesecloth set over a large pitcher. Squeeze out the liquid.

Storage: Place in an airtight container and refrigerate for 5 to 7 days.

Recipe Tip: For coffee creamer, I only add 4 cups of water, but for all of my other milk needs I add 6 cups of water to stretch the nuts as far as they can go.

If you want a flavored Nut Milk, try adding in a bit of any or all of the following: maple syrup, dates, sea salt, vanilla, cinnamon, or cocoa powder. Yum!

Hemp Milk

Nut-Free, Soy-Free

Hemp Milk is a great source of fiber, protein, and omega fatty acids that is nut-free! It tastes slightly earthy and has a great creamy consistency. The best part is that soaking is not required!

Preparation time: 10 minutes
Cooking time: 0 minutes
Servings: 2 pints
Ingredients
1 cup hemp hearts
4 cups filtered water
Directions:

In a high-speed blender, process the hemp hearts and water for 2 minutes.

Set cheesecloth or a nut milk bag over a pitcher, and pour the milk into it.

Storage: Place in an airtight container in the refrigerator for 5 to 7 days.

Recipe Tip: Because hemp hearts don't have skin, there really is no need to strain every time. But if you're going to be using Hemp Milk in another recipe application that requires a smooth final product, like most cheese, then I would still recommend it.

Coconut Yogurt

Nut-Free, Seed-Free, Soy-Free

Coconut Yogurt became a staple in my kitchen shortly after its debut appearance. I was amazed at how simple it was—using just two ingredients— and how tangy it came out after the fermentation process. It can be used in so many preparations, and as you will find in this book, it can bring vegan cheese to the next level. Learn this recipe and your dairy-free horizons will expand.

Preparation time: 24 hours
Cooking time: 0 minutes
Servings: 1 pint
Active time: 12 minutes
Inactive Time: 24 hours to ferment, 20 minutes to chill
Ingredients
1 (13.6-ounce) can extra-rich coconut milk

1 Lactobacillus probiotic capsule

Directions:

In a glass jar, combine the coconut milk and the contents of the probiotic capsule, discarding the capsule. Stir with a wooden spoon to combine.

Top the lid with cheesecloth, about four layers thick, and secure with a string.

Leave at room temperature for 24 hours so the yogurt ferments.

Refrigerate for at least 20 minutes before serving.

Storage: Place the jar in the refrigerator for up to 5 days.

Recipe Tip: If a thick Greek-style yogurt is what you're looking for, scrape off the thicker coconut cream that forms at the top of the can to use and leave out the thin liquid at the bottom. In this case, you will need 2 cans to make the same amount of yogurt.

Quinoa Rejuvelac

Nut-Free, Seed-Free, Soy-Free

Rejuvelac is a magical liquid that's created when you soak whole grains. The sprouting process creates a bit of fermentation in the water, and that water is what's used to flavor and further ferment many artisan vegan cheeses. You can also drink this on its own for probiotic health benefits. Using quinoa in this ferment produces a lemony, floral, and effervescent taste.

Preparation time: 3 days and 6 hours
Cooking time: 0 minutes
Servings: 1 pint
Active Time: 12 Minutes
Inactive Time: 3 To 4 Days
Ingredients
½ cup quinoa
Directions:

Rinse and drain the quinoa, and then place in a glass jar and cover with water by 1 inch. Cover with a cheesecloth and secure tightly with a string.

Leave overnight to sprout. If the grains don't sprout overnight, drain and rinse the quinoa, and let sit for another 4 to 6 hours, moist but not submerged in water.

Repeat the rinse a few times a day until the grains sprout.

Once the quinoa has sprouted, place it back in the glass jar and cover it with 2 cups of filtered water. Cover with cheesecloth and secure tightly with a string. Place in a cool dry place for 2 to 3

days until it develops a tangy flavor and smell. Strain the liquid from the quinoa, discarding (or reusing) the quinoa.

Storage: Place in an airtight container and refrigerate for up to 7 days.

Recipe Tip: You can make a second batch using the same quinoa and covering it with 2 cups of water again!

Barley Rejuvelac

Nut-Free, Seed-Free, Soy-Free

Using barley as the grain for rejuvelac produces a musky, earthy flavor that goes great in some of the richer, funkier cheeses.

Preparation time: 3 days and 6 hours
Cooking time: 0 minutes
Servings: 1 pint
Active Time: 12 minutes
Inactive Time: 3 to 4 days
Ingredients
½ cup barley
Directions:

Rinse and drain the barley, and then place in a glass jar and cover with water by 1 inch. Cover with a cheesecloth and secure tightly with a string.

Leave overnight to sprout. If the grains don't sprout overnight, drain the barley and let sit for another 4 to 6 hours, moist but not submerged in water.

Repeat the rinse a few times a day until the grains sprout.

Once the barley has sprouted, place it back in the glass jar and cover with 2 cups of filtered water. Cover with cheesecloth and secure tightly with a string. Place in a cool dry place for 2 to 3 days until it develops a tangy flavor and smell. Strain the liquid from the barley, discarding the barley.

Storage: Place in an airtight container and refrigerate for 7 days.

Recipe Tip: If white clouds appear on the surface of the liquid, scrape them off. This is not a bad thing, but if left unchecked, it can add bitterness to the final product.

Flavor Boosters (Fish Glazes, Meat Rubs & Fish Rubs)

Classic Honey Mustard Fish Glaze

Complement your choice of fish including salmon by infusing it with succulent flavors and a perfectly glazed look by this classic honey mustard glaze.

Honey and mustard are versatile and fun, as they let you experiment endlessly and discover something new every time.

Preparation Time: 5 min.
Cooking Time: 5 min.
Servings: 1/2 cup/4 oz.
Ingredients:
Dijon mustard - 2 tsp.
Soy sauce (low sodium) - 4 tbsp.
Honey - 6 tbsp.
Lime juice - 2 tsp.
Directions:

To make the honey mustard fish glaze, combine the mustard, soy sauce, lime juice, and honey in your medium-sized bowl. Gently blend the ingredients.

Then, add the mixture into your medium-sized saucepan. Let the mixture simmer gradually for about 2 minutes.

Now, take your favorite cooked/grilled/baked salmon or any other fish variety. Gently spread or pour the prepared glaze over the fish/salmon. Allow a few minutes for the glaze to set in. Enjoy the mustard glazed fish meal!

Maple Syrup Spiced Fish Glaze

Give your parties and occasions a rich and classic upgrade with this maple syrup glaze. Nutmeg, combined with sharp flavors of cinnamon, makes this yummy fish glaze perfect to prepare holiday or seasonal meals.

Preparation Time: 5 min.
Cooking Time: 5 min.
Servings: 1 cup/8 oz.
Ingredients:
Apple cider vinegar - 1/2 cup
Apple cider - 1/2 cup
Olive oil - 1 tbs.
Brown sugar - 2 tbs.
Maple syrup - 1 tbs.
Cinnamon - 2 tsp.
Salt - 1 tsp.
Nutmeg - 1 tsp.
Onion powder - 1/2 tsp.
Directions:

To make the maple syrup glaze, combine all mentioned fish marinade ingredients in your food processor or blender. Gently blend the ingredients.

Now, take your favorite cooked/grilled/baked baked salmon or any other fish variety. Gently spread or pour the prepared glaze over the cuts. Allow a few minutes for the glaze to set in. Enjoy the maple syrup-glazed fish meal!

Teriyaki Tangy Fish Glaze

Rice wine paired with tangy orange juice make it a perfect fish meal to have on any given day. This saucy Teriyaki glaze brings out the juicy, mild flavors of fish. Try out this on weekend and impress yourself!

Preparation Time: 5 min.
Cooking Time: 5 min.
Servings: 1 ¼ cup/10 oz.
Ingredients:
Rice wine - 1/4 cup
Orange juice, with pulp - 3/4 cup
Soy sauce - 3 tbs.
Minced scallions - 1 tbs.
Honey - 1 tbs.
Orange slices – for garnishing
Lemon juice - 1 tsp.
Directions:

To make the teriyaki glaze, combine the mentioned fish marinade ingredients in your food processor or blender. Gently blend the ingredients.

Now, take your favorite cooked/grilled/baked baked salmon or any other fish variety. Gently spread or pour the prepared glaze over the cuts. Allow a few minutes for the glaze to set in. Enjoy the teriyaki glazed fish meal!

Extra Scrumptious Super Meat & Fish Rubs

Spice up your dream meats and fish with some extra flavors of the following handpicked collection of meat as well as fish rubs to put an end to your spicy food cravings.

Rubs – How Much is Adequate for your Meat?

For meat cuts including steak, chicken, and pork, using rub mixture of 1 tbs. (3 tsp.) per 16 oz. piece is suggested.

For variety of fish, rub mixture of ½ tbs. (1 to 2 tsp.) to 1 tbs. (3 tsp.) per 16 oz. piece is adequate.

To be safe, use less quantity for the first time to determine its spice strength. You will be able to adjust the quantity next time.

Tunisian Mixed Spiced Rub

This incredible rub recipe hailed from the Tunisian cooking secrets; the rub is the essential seasoning base for variety of Tunisian dishes.

This lovely spice blend created by caraway seeds, coriander, and hot pepper works like a charm on your favorite pork tenderloin, chicken as well as salmon.

Preparation Time: 5 min.
Cooking Time: 5 min.
Servings: 5-½ tsp.
Ingredients:
Coriander seeds - 2 tsp.
Caraway seeds - 2 tsp.
Crushed red pepper - 3/4 tsp.
Garlic powder - 3/4 tsp.
Kosher salt - 1/2 tsp.
Directions:

Mix in the coriander seeds, red pepper and caraway seeds in your spice blender, grinder or processor to make this rub. Start processing or blending the mixed spices on "pulse" mode mixture to ground.

Put the mixed spice mixture into a bowl; mix in the salt and garlic powder. Mix again well.

Now, take your choice of meat cut and place it on a firm surface. Brush or rub the freshly made rub on it; pat gently for the rub to stick onto the surface. Turn the meat cut and repeat to spice up its other side. Repeat with other meat cuts.

The freshly rubbed meat is ready to be grilled or cooked!

All Purpose Dill Seed Rub

Boost your steak with vibrant, spiced flavors of this all-purpose dill seed rub. It also beautifully seasons chicken and pork meat cuts. Apply this unique rub minutes before grilling or cooking; you can also store it at room temperature for 12-14 days without sacrificing on its quality.

Preparation Time: 5 min.
Cooking Time: 5 min.
Servings: 6-7 tsp.
Ingredients:
Paprika - 2 tsp.
Ground coriander - 2 tsp.
Dill seed – 1 tsp.
Dry mustard - ½ tsp.
Garlic, minced – 1 clove
Black pepper and salt as required
Cayenne pepper - ¼ tsp.
Directions:

Mix in all the rub ingredients in your mixing bowl to make the dill seed rub. Gently mix all ingredients using spatula or spoon to form an aromatic rub mixture.

Now, take your choice of meat cut and place it on a firm surface. Brush the freshly made rub on it; pat gently for the rub to stick onto the surface. Turn the meat cut and repeat to spice up its other side. Repeat with other meat cuts.

Let your meat cuts adequately season for more rich flavors for a few hours in your refrigerator. Take them out, as they are ready to be cooked or grilled!

Rosemary Thyme Rub

This special rub recipe represents an interesting balance of spicy and sweet flavors to make truly mesmerizing meat meals.

A spiced combo of rosemary, thyme, and celery seeds never fails to produce delicious dishes with well-balanced flavors for the whole family.

Preparation Time: 5 min.
Cooking Time: 5 min.
Servings: 1 cup/16 tbs.
Ingredients:
Dried thyme - 1/4 cup
Dried crushed rosemary - 1/4 cup
Dry mustard - 2 tbs.
Ground black pepper - 4 tsp.
Salt - 4 tsp.
Onion powder - 4 tsp.
Ground cloves - 2 tsp.
Celery seed - 2 tsp.
Cayenne- 1 tsp.
Directions:

Mix in all mentioned rub ingredients in your mixing bowl to make the rosemary rub. Gently mix all ingredients using spatula or spoon to form an aromatic rub mixture.

Now, take your choice of meat cut and place it on a firm surface. Brush the freshly made rub on it; pat gently for the rub to stick onto the surface. Turn the meat cut and repeat to spice up its other side. Repeat with other meat cuts.

Let your meat cuts adequately season for more rich flavors for a few hours in your refrigerator. Take them out, as they are ready to be cooked or grilled!

Super Spiced Curry Rub

Your favorite meat cuts deserve a little jazzing up with this unique curry flavored rub. Paprika mixed with curry powder and cinnamon creates a perfect blend of spices. Be creative and add one or two of your favorite spices in it to come up with your own special version of spiced curry rub.

Preparation Time: 5 min.
Cooking Time: 5 min.
Yield: 10 tbs.
Ingredients:
Ground ginger - 2 tbs.
Yellow curry powder - 3 tbs.
Ground cinnamon - 2 tbs.
Salt - 1 tsp.
Mild paprika - 1 tbs.
Ground cumin - 2 tbs.
Ground allspice - 1 tsp.

Directions:
One by one, mix in all mentioned rub ingredients in your mixing bowl to make the curry rub. Gently mix all the ingredients using spatula or spoon to form an aromatic rub mixture.

Now, take your choice of meat cut and place it on a firm surface. Brush or rub the freshly made rub on it; pat gently for the rub to stick to the surface. Turn the meat cut and repeat to spice up its other side. Repeat with other meat cuts.

Let your meat cuts adequately season for more rich flavors for a few hours in your refrigerator. Take them out, as they are ready to be cooked or grilled!

Mexican Cocoa Rub

Want to spice up your dry meats with savory Mexican flavors? Try out my classy rub this weekend. Cocoa and espresso powder are a special addition to this Mexican style rub creating soothing spiced aroma.

Preparation Time: 5 min.
Cooking Time: 5 min.
Servings: 9 tsp.
Ingredients:
Water – 1 tbs.
Cocoa, unsweetened – 1 tsp.
Instant espresso powder – 2 tsp.
Smoked paprika – 2 tsp.
Olive oil – 1 tsp.
Ground cumin – 1 tsp.
Salt – ¼ tsp.
Directions:
One by one, mix in all the ingredients in your mixing bowl to make the cocoa rub. Gently mix all the ingredients using spatula or spoon to form an aromatic rub mixture.

Now, take your choice of meat cut and place it on a firm surface. Brush or rub the freshly made rub on it; pat gently for the rub to stick to the surface. Turn the meat cut and repeat to spice up its other side. Repeat with other meat cuts.

Let your meat cuts adequately season for more rich flavors for a few hours in your refrigerator. Take them out, as they are ready to be cooked or grilled!

Juniper Sage Meat Rub

This unique meat rub has been crafted with quality by including numerous healthy herbs such as juniper berries, lay leaf, red pepper, etc. It delivers piney accent to the rub, which ultimately enhances the flavor of your favorite meat cuts.

Preparation Time: 5 min.
Cooking Time: 5 min.
Servings: 8 tsp.
Ingredients:

Bay leaf - 1
Black peppercorns - 1 tsp.
Juniper berries - 2 tsp.
Extra-virgin olive oil - 2 tbs.
Crushed red pepper - ½ tsp.
Kosher salt - ½ tsp.
Minced garlic – 1 clove
Minced sage leaves – 6
Directions:

Mix in the bay leaf, red pepper, salt, peppercorns, and berries in your spice blender, grinder or processor to make the juniper rub. Start processing or grinding the mixed spiced on "pulse" mode to ground.

Empty the mixed spice mixture in a bowl; mix in the sage leaves, oil, and garlic. Mix again well.

Now, take your choice of meat cut and place it on a firm surface. Brush or rub the freshly made rub on it; pat gently for the rub to stick to the surface. Turn the meat cut and repeat to spice up its other side. Repeat with other meat cuts.

The freshly rubbed meat is ready to be grilled or cooked!

Southwestern Oregano Thyme Rub

This rub is a perfect blend of herbal, sweet, and earthy ingredients to make your day truly special and delicious. If you wish to make your meat cuts less spicy, then you can adjust the quantity of chili powder.

Preparation Time: 5 min.
Cooking Time: 5 min.
Servings: 11 tbs.
Ingredients:
Garlic powder - 2 tbs.
Chili powder - 2 tbs.
Dry mustard - 2 tbs.
Dried thyme- 1 tbs.
Dried oregano - 1 tbs.
Mild paprika - 1 tbs.
Ground coriander - 1 tbs.
Ground cumin - 1 tbs.
Salt - 2 tsp.
Directions:

Mix all mentioned ingredients in your mixing bowl to make the oregano thyme rub. Gently mix all the ingredients using spatula or spoon to form an aromatic rub mixture.

Now, take your choice of meat cut and place it on a firm surface. Brush or rub the freshly made rub on it; pat gently for the rub to stick onto the surface. Turn the meat cut and repeat to spice up its other side. Repeat with other meat cuts.

The freshly rubbed meat is ready to be grilled or cooked!

Tangy Pepper & Thyme Rub

Transform your dry meats into full of citrusy, dark, and spicy flavors with this triple spice rub. The tangy thyme rub is quite easy to prepare and beautifully spices up your chicken, pork as well as beef.

Preparation Time: 5 min.
Cooking Time: 0 min.
Servings: 2 tbs.
Ingredients:
Dried thyme - 1tbs.
Lime zest, finely grated – 1 tbs.
Sea salt and black pepper as required
Directions:

Mix in all the ingredients in your mixing bowl to make the pepper and thyme rub. Gently mix all the ingredients using spatula or spoon to form an aromatic rub mixture.

Now, take your choice of meat cut and place it on a firm surface. Brush or rub the freshly made rub on it; pat gently for the rub to stick onto the surface. Turn the meat cut and repeat to spice up its other side. Repeat with other meat cuts.

The freshly rubbed meat is ready to be grilled or cooked!

Oregano Cumin Tilapia Rub

This rub is a family-friendly way to savor an earthy, mild combination of spices in your favorite fish meals. The rub includes mild flavors, suitable even for children. Apart from Tilapia, it is also perfect for varieties of fish including salmon. Enjoy with mashed potatoes!

Preparation Time: 5 min.
Cooking Time: 5 min.
Servings: 4-5 tsp.
Ingredients:
Light brown sugar – 1 1/2 tsp.
Paprika – 1 1/2 tsp.
Dried oregano - 1 tsp.
Cumin - 1/2 tsp.
Garlic powder - 3/4 tsp.
Cayenne pepper - 1/4 tsp.
Salt - 1 tsp.
Directions:

Mix in all mentioned ingredients in your mixing bowl to make the cumin tilapia rub. Gently mix all the ingredients using spatula or spoon to form an aromatic rub mixture.

Now, take your choice of fish and place it on a firm surface. Brush or rub the freshly made rub on it; pat gently for the rub to stick on the surface. Turn it and repeat to spice up its other side.

Let your fish cuts adequately season for more rich flavors for some time in your refrigerator.

*Do not let your fish season for more than 2 hours (but not less than 30 minutes).

Take it out, as it is ready to be cooked or grilled!

Spicy Sumac Rub

This special spicy rub perfectly complements different choices of fish; it adds up extra flavors to your fish-based meals. I mean, no one likes to compromise on the mild, mouth-watering taste of Tilapia.

Preparation Time: 5 min.
Cooking Time: 5 min.
Servings: 2-3 tsp.
Ingredients:
Dried thyme - 1/2 tsp.
Powdered sumac - 1/2 tsp.
Any variety of Creole seasoning - 1/2 tsp.
Onion powder - 1/4 tsp.
Garlic powder - 1/4 tsp.
Salt - 1/4 tsp.
Directions:
Mix all mentioned ingredients in your mixing bowl to make the spicy sumac rub. Gently mix all ingredients using spatula or spoon to form an aromatic rub mixture.

Now, take your choice of fish and place it on a firm surface. Brush or rub the freshly made rub on it; pat gently for the rub to stick onto the surface. Turn it and repeat to spice up its other side.

Let your fish cuts adequately season for more rich flavors for some time in your refrigerator.

*Do not let your fish season for more than 2 hours (but not less than 30 minutes).

Take it out, as it is ready to be cooked or grilled!

Lemon Pepper Coriander Rub

This intelligently created pepper coriander rub provides hints of tartness along with mild spiciness with inclusion of chili powder. A great choice of rub to flavor-up your weekend nights as well as any night you wish to make special.

Partner your fish meals prepared with this special rub with red wine for a truly refreshing meal time.

Preparation Time: 5 min.
Cooking Time: 5 min.
Servings: ½ cup + 3 tsp.
Ingredients:
Chili powder - 1 tbsp.
Lemon pepper seasoning - 1/4 cup
Ground cumin - 1 tbsp.
Light brown sugar, firmly packed - 1 1/2 tsp.
Ground coriander - 1 tbsp.
Kosher salt - 1/2 tsp.
Ground black pepper - 1 1/4 tsp.
Red pepper flakes - 1/2 tsp.
Directions:
Mix in all mentioned ingredients in your mixing bowl to make the lemon coriander rub. Gently mix all the ingredients using spatula or spoon to form an aromatic rub mixture.

Now, take your choice of fish and place it on a firm surface. Brush or rub the freshly made rub on it; pat gently for the rub onto stick on the surface. Turn it and repeat to spice up its other side.

Let your fish cuts adequately season for more rich flavors for some time in your refrigerator.

*Do not let your fish season for more than 2 hours (but not less than 30 minutes).

Take it out, as it is ready to be cooked or grilled!

Long Island Spiced Rub

Tickle your taste buds with a vibrant spice mixture of cinnamon, nutmeg, black pepper, and cloves. Fish meals spiced with this rub make perfect combo with your choice of fresh salad along with lime drink or juice; it is also a great choice to pair up with coconut and pineapple salsa.

Preparation Time: 5 min.
Cooking Time: 5 min.
Servings: 16-18 tsp.
Ingredients:
Nutmeg - 2 tsp.
All-spice - 1 tbsp.
Cinnamon - 2 tsp.
Ground ginger - 2 tsp.
Garlic powder - 2 tsp.
Ground black pepper - 2 tsp.
Ground cloves - 1 tsp.
Cayenne pepper - 2 tsp.
Sugar - 1½ tbsp.
Salt - 1½ tbsp.
Directions:
Mix in all mentioned ingredients in your mixing bowl to make the long island rub. Gently mix all

ingredients using spatula or spoon to form an aromatic rub mixture.

Now, take your choice of fish and place it on a firm surface. Brush or rub the freshly made rub on it; pat gently for the rub onto stick on the surface. Turn it and repeat to spice up its other side. Let your fish cuts adequately season for more rich flavors for some time in your refrigerator.

*Do not let your fish season for more than 2 hours (but not less than 30 minutes).

Take it out, as it is ready to be cooked or grilled!

Sauce Recipes

Runner Recovery Bites

Preparation time: 10 minutes
Cooking time: 10 minutes
Servings: 12
Ingredients:
1/4 cup pumpkin seeds, soaked for 1 hour
1/3 cup oats
1/4 cup sunflower seeds, soaked for 1 hour
5 dates
1 teaspoon maca powder
1 tablespoon goji berries
1 teaspoon coconut, shredded and unsweetened
1 tablespoon coconut water
1 teaspoon vanilla extract
1 tablespoon protein powder
1 tablespoon maple syrup
1/4 cup hemp seeds
A pinch sea salt

Directions:
Drain sunflower and pumpkin seeds and add to a blender. Blend until a paste forms. Add dates and blend to mix. Add the remaining ingredients except hemp seeds and blend until a dough forms.
Roll 1 tablespoon dough into balls with hands. Roll the ball in hemp seeds until covered.
Transfer the prepared balls to a plate and freeze until firm.
Serve and enjoy.

High Protein Vegan Cheesy Sauce

Preparation time: 10 minutes
Cooking time: 10 minutes
Servings: 2 cups
Ingredients:
1 1/4 cups unsweetened plant-based milk
1 block tofu
1 teaspoon onion powder
2 teaspoon garlic powder
1/2 cup nutritional yeast
1/4 teaspoon turmeric
3/4 teaspoon salt
Directions:
Add all ingredients to a blender and blend until smooth. Combine well. Add more milk as desired.
Refrigerate for 24 hours.
Serve and enjoy.

Vegan High-Protein Queso

Preparation time: 5 minutes
Cooking time: 5 minutes
Servings: 2
Ingredients:
1/4 cup nutritional yeast
1/2 block tofu
3 tablespoon lemon juice
1/4 teaspoon tapioca starch
1/4 teaspoon garlic powder
1/4 teaspoon turmeric
1/4 teaspoon onion powder
1/4 cup water
1/2 teaspoon salt
Directions:
Add tofu, yeast, starch, lemon juice, salt, garlic powder, turmeric and onion powder and blend until well mixed.
Add water as desired. Heat in a microwave for 30 seconds.
Serve and enjoy.

Vegan Buffalo Sauce

Preparation time: 5 minutes
Cooking time: 5 minutes
Servings: 1 cup
Ingredients:
1/2 cup soy milk

1 cup hot sauce
1/2 cup vinegar
1/2 teaspoon pepper
2 tablespoons sugar
1/2 teaspoon garlic granules
1 tablespoon tomato sauce

Directions:

Mix soy milk, hot sauce, sugar, vinegar, sugar, pepper, tomato sauce and garlic granules in a pan and cook over medium heat for 10 minutes.

Let cool and serve.

Vegan Ranch Dressing (Dipping Sauce)

Preparation time: 5 minutes
Cooking time: 5 minutes
Servings: 8
Ingredients:
2 tablespoons lemon juice
14 oz. silken tofu
1 tablespoon yellow mustard
1 tablespoon apple cider vinegar
1 teaspoon onion granules
1 tablespoon agave
1 teaspoon garlic granules
2 tablespoons parsley, minced
2 tablespoons dill, minced
1/2 teaspoon Himalayan salt
Directions:

Add all ingredients except parsley and dill to a blender and blend until smooth at high speed.

Add dill and parsley and blend until mixed.
Serve chilled.

Vegan Smokey Maple BBQ Sauce

Preparation time: 5 minutes
Cooking time: 5 minutes
Servings: 8
Ingredients:
1 tablespoon maple syrup
1/2 cup ketchup
1 teaspoon garlic powder
1 teaspoon liquid smoke
Directions:

Add all ingredients to a bowl. Mix them until well combined.

Serve and enjoy.

Vegan White Bean Gravy

Preparation time: 5 minutes
Cooking time: 5 minutes
Servings: 2 1/5 cups
Ingredients:
1 cup of soy milk
1 cup vegetable broth
1 cup white beans, rinsed and drained
1 tablespoon nutritional yeast
3 tablespoons tamari
1 teaspoon garlic granules, dried
2 teaspoons onion granules, dried
2 tablespoons all-purpose flour
1 tablespoon combination thyme, oregano, dill, minced
1/4 teaspoon black pepper
1/4 teaspoon Himalayan salt
Directions:

Add all ingredients except flour, herbs, and salt to a blender and blend on high speed until smooth.

Add this mixture to a pan placed over medium heat. Add salt, herbs, and flour, whisk all the time — Cook for 5 minutes.

Serve and enjoy.

Tahini Maple Dressing

Preparation time: 5 minutes
Cooking time: 5 minutes
Servings: 4 oz
Ingredients
¼ cup tahini
1 ½ tablespoons maple syrup
2 teaspoons lemon juice
¼ cup of water
1/8 teaspoon Himalayan pink salt
Directions:

Add all the ingredients to a bowl, Stir well to combine, until well mixed.

Use as a dressing for the salad or other dishes. Store in a fridge.

Coconut Sugar Peanut Sauce

Preparation time: 5 minutes
Cooking time: 5 minute
Servings: 1 ½ cups
Ingredients
4 tablespoons coconut sugar

6 tablespoons powdered peanut butter
1 tablespoon chili sauce
2 tablespoons liquid aminos
¼ cup of water
1 teaspoon lime juice
½ teaspoon ginger powder
Directions:
In a bowl, combine all the ingredients until properly combined. Serve as a topping for the salad or other dishes.
Store in a fridge.

Coconut Sauce

Preparation time: 15 minutes
Cooking time: 15 minutes
Servings: 3
Ingredients
½ cup red lentils, cooked
4 carrots, peeled, chopped
1 cup (250 ml) coconut milk, canned
3 tablespoons nutritional yeast
½ onion, diced
2 garlic cloves, minced
Pepper and salt, to taste

Directions:
Boil the carrots for 10 minutes in a pan.
Blend the cooked carrots, lentils, onion, garlic, yeast and coconut milk in a blender until smooth. Stir in pepper and salt.
Pour the mixture into a saucepan and cook for 2 minutes, stirring frequently.
Pour the sauce over the cooked pasta or salad servers.

Vegan Bean Pesto

Preparation time: 5 minutes
Cooking time: 5 minutes
Servings: 2
Ingredients
1 can (15 oz.) white beans, drained, rinsed
2 cups basil leaves, washed, dried
½ cup non-dairy milk
2 tablespoons olive oil
3 tablespoons nutritional yeast
1 garlic clove, peeled
Pepper and salt to taste
Directions:
Blend all the ingredients (except the seasonings) in a blender until smooth.
Sprinkle with pepper and salt to taste, then blend for 1 extra minute. Enjoy with pasta.

Conclusion

I want to thank you once again for choosing this book. I hope it proved to be an informative read.

A plant-based diet primarily involves consuming foods that are entirely derived from plants. The primary idea of this diet is to increase your consumption of healthy and wholesome foods while eliminating processed foods. By now, you have realized the various benefits this diet offers. By increasing your consumption of the different plant-based foods mentioned in this book, you can attain your weight-loss objectives, improve your overall health, and reduce your risk of developing several serious illnesses.

Now, you just need to stock up your pantry with the required ingredients mentioned in the food list in this book. By concentrating on certain anti-inflammatory foods, you can tackle inflammation effectively. All the recipes given in this book are easy to prepare, tasty and healthy. Use the various plant-based alternatives to the regular foods you consume, and you won't feel like you're missing out on anything.

If you're excited to get started with a plant-based diet, use the 21-day meal plan provided in this book to plan out all your meals. Cooking has never been this easy! You don't need to compromise your taste buds for the sake of your health. By following a plant-based diet, you can effectively eat your way to better health.

So, what are you waiting for? Let's get rustling in the kitchen.

Thank you, and all the best.

Made in the USA
Monee, IL
01 August 2022

10703115R00070